MAKING OF AMERICA

SERIES

GRAVESEND

THE HOME OF CONEY ISLAND

DEDICATED

TO

JASON PHILIP CARO

CONEY ISLAND, 1923. People on Steeplechase Pier enjoy the view of the bathers on Sunday, May 20, 1923.

THE
MAKING OF AMERICA
SERIES

GRAVESEND

THE HOME OF CONEY ISLAND

ERIC J. IERARDI

ARCADIA

ISBN 0-7385-2361-5

Published by Arcadia Publishing,
an imprint of Tempus Publishing, Inc.
2 Cumberland Street
Charleston, SC 29401

Printed in Great Britain.

Library of Congress Catalog Card Number: 2001091016

For all general information contact Arcadia Publishing at:
Telephone 843-853-2070
Fax 843-853-0044
E-Mail sales@arcadiapublishing.com

For customer service and orders:
Toll-Free 1-888-313-2665

Visit us on the Internet at http://www.arcadiapublishing.com

All photographs, illustrations, etc., except where marked, are from the private collection of Eric J. Ierardi and the Gravesend Historical Society.

CONTENTS

ACKNOWLEDGMENTS

Poet John Donne said, "No man is an island, entire of itself." When one sets pen to paper, the author reflects on those who have helped to bring the undertaking about. As I commence the drama of Gravesend, I think of those who helped bring this tale of one town into reality. First and foremost, to my parents, Angelina and Joseph Ierardi, for not only putting up with cluttered rooms, but whose patience, understanding, and support through years of research made this project possible.

Special appreciation goes to the following: the Brooklyn Historical Society, the Brooklyn Public Library System, Mr. and Mrs. Vincenzo Gattabria, Rolf C. Graeber, the Gravesend Historical Society of England, the James A. Kelly Local Historical Studies Institute, Professor Arthur Konop, Dr. Louis D. Fontana, Honorable Sebastian Leone, the Office of the Brooklyn Borough President, David G. Oats, Dr. Joseph Palisi, Dr. John Tantillo, and the New York Racing Association.

INTRODUCTION

Throughout most of my life, I always wanted to write about the historic area in which I grew up. As a child, I remember the first time I learned about Gravesend and Coney Island. While attending class at S.S. Simon and Jude School, I recall the time when I was up at the blackboard writing. Another student was talking to the teacher about "this old historic cemetery not more than a block away from the school." I naturally heard what was being talked about, and dropping what I was doing, screamed out, "What cemetery?" in full voice. My reaction was a bit unorthodox, and the entire class laughed while I was being reprimanded.

From that moment on, my love for local history began. Into the annals of Gravesend's and Coney Island's past I ventured. Talk of Indians and English settlers became reality as I searched through primary source materials. Amusement parks, racetracks, and huge hotels accommodating hundreds were pieces of the puzzle that were now falling into place. Fun times, laughs, and thrills, as well as corruption and bribery, were all part of the facts of life of the area.

What you are about to read is the story of a town whose beginning was founded on religious freedom and city planning; a town whose founder was a woman. To make this reading experience more enjoyable, I will recount some stories from the original town records that will enlighten you as to the type of life the early settlers experienced; you will be amazed at the lifestyle of these early adventures—a psychologist's and sociologist's paradise!

Gravesend not only included the small village area of Gravesend, but also Coney Island, Sheepshead Bay, and a part of Bensonhurst, as well as many other areas in Brooklyn. It will be apparent to you as you read, that these early settlers had established three goals. First, they wanted to organize a town; second, they wanted to live in peace; and third, they wanted their own town to prosper and grow. It grew as centuries passed, and with its growth came new faces, new ideas, and a new way to view life. From Dutch to English to the present-day conglomeration of America—Voila Gravesend! Viva Gravesend!

1. EARLY EXPLORATION

As the morning of September 8, 1609, dawned, the crew of the *Half Moon* eyed from their deck the desolate, forbidding, white sandy beach to the port side. Their small craft had entered a great harbor, which closed around them and beckoned forward to the mouths of two rivers. Captain Henry Hudson anchored and dispatched a landing party to the beach, which was alive with activity. A number of bronzed natives, some dressed in loin cloths, waved excitedly. Cautiously, the oarsmen pulled toward the breaking surf and with a scraping of the boat's bottom on the fine, clean sand, the first white Europeans set foot on what was later to be known as the "Playground of the World"—Coney Island.

The explorer Hudson described his first encounter with the natives, "They came aboored of us, seeming very glad of our comming, and brought greene tobacco, and gave us of it for knives and beads." As to their appearance, the *Half Moon*'s log discloses, "They grease their bodies and hair very often and paint their faces with several colours, as black, white, red, yellow, blue, etc., which they take great pride in, everyone being painted in a several manner." They were further described as "very civill" and in stature "tall, straight, muscular and agile."

An ecological paradise, the waters around the island abounded with numerous species of fish. "Our boate went on land with our net to fish," reads Hudson's journal, "and caught ten great mullets, of a foote and a halfe long a Piece, and a ray as great as foure men could hale into a ship."

Upon landing, Hudson noticed that the island was hopping with a multitude of rabbits, and seeing them, he named the island "Coney," an Old English word meaning rabbit. The name was corrupted into "Conyen Eylandt" by the Dutch, "Cunny Island" (showing the early pronunciation), and "Conyne Island"; all variations of Coney.

A romanticized version proposed by some historians is derived from Robert Juet, Hudson's mate who wrote the following in his notebook:

HENRY HUDSON. This famed New World explorer led one of the first expeditions into the general area of Long Island.

As they came back, they were set upon by two [Indian] canoes, the one having twelve, the other fourteen men. The night came on, and it began to rayne, so that their Match [to fire the gun] went out; and they had one man slaine in the fight, which was an Englishman, named John Colman, with an Arrow shot into his throat, and two more hurt. . . . It grew so dark that they could not find the ship [*Half Moon*] that night, but labored to and fro on their Oares . . . the seventh, was faire, and by ten of the clocke they returned aboard the ship, and brought our dead man with them, whom we carryed on Land and buryed.

Legend has it that John Coleman was buried on the site where the Half Moon Hotel was built some 300 years later and the island's name was a corruption of his last name.

Hudson, an Englishman sailing for the Dutch East India Company, failed to realize that the Indians were very protective of their land, especially of their beaches. The beach was their treasury. Along the white expanses the Indians searched and collected sewan, or wampum, which were shells that were used as money. With the sewan the Indian was able to trade and bargain with neighboring tribes or with the whites.

After a short stay, Hudson continued up the river that today is named in his honor. He navigated to approximately the site of Albany before returning to the Great Bay. His discovery of this navigable river and land was to be of the greatest importance to the Dutch merchants and ship captains who were to follow.

Eighty-five years prior to Hudson's arrival came another ship and another master navigator. The ship was *La Dauphine*; the navigator, Giovanni da Verrazzano. Verrazzano, a Florentine by birth, was employed by the French monarch Francis I. Verrazzano was the first to sail into New York Harbor, and was the first to view the land he called "Angouleme," after the family name of Francis I. In 1527, Vesconte de Maggilo of Genoa depicted the site of the great harbor and its rivers on his world map. Thus, New York received its first name by its first European visitor.

On the April 17, 1524, Verrazzano anchored his caravel in the Narrows. Today, the great steel arch spanning that body of water bears his name. Verrazzano described the discovery as follows:

> But because we rode at anchor in a place well fenced from the wind, we could not venture ourselves without knowledge of the place, and we passed up with our boat only into the said river, and saw the country very well peopled. The people are almost like unto the others, and clad with feathers of fowls of divers colors. They came towards us very cheerfully, making great shouts of admiration, showing us where we might come to land most safely with our boat. We entered up the said river into the land about half a league, where it made a most pleasant lake about 3 leagues in compass; on the which they rowed from the one side to the other, to the number of 30 of their small boats, wherein were many people, which passed from one shore to the other to come and see us. And behold, upon the sudden (as it is wont to fall out in sailing) a contrary flaw of wind coming from the sea, we were enforced to return to our ship, leaving this land, to our great discontentment for the great commodity and pleasantness thereof, which we suppose is not without some riches, all the hills showing mineral matters in them.

Verrazzano prudently anchored his ship far out in the deep waters. The treacherous currents could have forced him aground and marooned the expedition. He believed that the Narrows were part of a river, and his reference to the "pleasant lake," which was about 10 miles in circumference, refers to New York's Upper Bay. He named the bay "Santa Margarita" in tribute to the king's sister, Marguerite, the duchess d'Alencon. *La Dauphine* sailed without incident, leaving the plush, verdant area that was to become one day the "Capital of the World."

During the seventeenth century, Holland was experiencing a period of great economic and social progress, a "golden age." The flag of the House of Orange flew from more masts than any other maritime power. Art and culture flourished as the wealth of the world was borne on the decks of Dutch ships back to the motherland. The entrepreneurial spirit of the Dutch businessman was piqued by reports from the early explorers of a land to the west rich in timber, minerals, and furs.

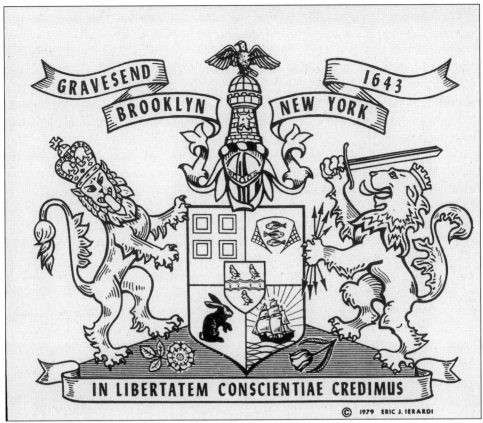

GRAVESEND'S COAT OF ARMS. Designed by Eric J. Ierardi, the town's coat of arms uses some major historic elements that are associated with the founding of the Town of Gravesend.

In time, other ships followed the footsteps of Henry Hudson. Ships would sail to the island between the East and Hudson Rivers successfully trading with the Indians, and return to Amsterdam with their holds loaded with rich furs and pelts. Stimulated by the profits of these enterprises, the Dutch merchants prepared two new departures. Captain Adrian Block and Captain Hendrick Christiaensen were to captain the *Tiger* and the *Fortune* to the New World.

In June 1613, Adrian Block, commanding the *Tiger*, and Hendrick Christiaensen, commanding the *Fortune*, left Amsterdam. By late summer, both ships sailed into the harbor of New York. Block anchored his ship off the tip of lower Manhattan, while Christiaensen sailed up the Hudson River for further exploration. Establishing trade with the Indians at a post he called Fort Orange, a site now the city of Albany, Christiaensen continued to probe the secrets of the river and its forbidding hills.

Laden with furs of otter, beaver, fox, and ermine (weasel), the *Tiger* prepared for the long voyage home. On the eve before the departure, a spark from a lamp, ignited and fanned by chilling November winds, erupted into a blazing holocaust,

11

setting the entire vessel aflame. Men scampered to subdue the flames but at best only some rope and sail could be jettisoned and saved. The ill-fated *Tiger* burned to the water line. Faces black with charcoal and soot watched as the flames enveloped their hope of returning to Holland.

The Werpoes, a local Indian tribe, who had befriended Block and his crew, assisted them in getting timbers to construct the first crude huts, and these marooned whites became Manhattan's first settlers. Block, with the industrial spirit that exemplifies the Dutch, set his crew to work building a new vessel. The new ship was constructed from wood of oak and hickory trees. It was nearly 45 feet in length, 11 feet wide, and 16 tons in weight. Christened the *Onrust*, or *Restless*, it was launched into the East River and was the first ship built in the New World by Europeans.

Up the river to a point where the waters churned white and the currents held unknown dangers, the dauntless survivors sailed their new charge. Block named the spot Helle-gatt (Hell Gate). Through a passage into a becalmed sound, the *Onrust* traveled its way. Charting the shores and islands (one he named for himself, Block Island), the captain mapped the Connecticut River and circumnavigated Long Island. Earlier maps had shown only an unbroken coast. Around Montauk Point and along the south shore, the craft put into a huge bay dotted with many islands and bars. The Indians of Jamaica Bay received the visitors hospitably, giving food and shelter to the white travelers.

Sailing back along the coast and up to Cape Cod, Block accidentally and fortuitously intercepted Christiaensen. The crew of the *Fortune* had also wintered in the unknown regions, and now that spring had returned and the North Atlantic was navigable, they made preparations for the crossing. Leaving Cornelius Hendricksen to command the *Onrust*, Block joined Christiaensen aboard the larger ship and set sail for Amsterdam, never to return to the land he did so much to reveal. For over 300 years, nothing except an innocuous passage in a history book alluded to the ill-fated *Tiger*.

In spring 1916, workmen engaged in the digging of the I.R.T. (Interboro Rapid Transit) subway line made a startling discovery. Beneath the turmoil of a burgeoning city, at the intersection of Greenwich and Dey Streets in lower Manhattan, shovels unearthed what appeared to be the prow of a ship. A young Irishman who was in charge of the "mucking crew" was summoned. Not a historian, James Kelly did possess a deep-seated love for history, and this appreciation of the past suggested to him the importance of this chance discovery. Searching for expert opinion, he requested assistance from the Museum of Natural History. After an on-the-spot investigation, it was generally conceded that the charred remains, found some three blocks from the water, was all that was left of Block's *Tiger*.

Kelly requested that the entire ship be unearthed, but delays on the job jeopardized the contract and the company issued orders that the impediment be severed and the rest be walled up. An 8-foot section of oaken timber was cut and the remainder deserted in its bed of charcoal and silt. The relic was moved to the old Battery Aquarium and set in the seal tank, where it served as an ornament for the sporting sea lions. Ignominiously, it was casually viewed by visitors for almost 30 years until fate intervened. By passage of a local law ordinance and with monies appropriated by the city council, the old aquarium was razed and a new modern sea museum constructed at Coney Island.

The years had been good to the young Irish lad, James Kelly. He had thrown in his lot with Jimmy Walker and ventured into politics. Appointed by Walker as first deputy county clerk of Kings County, Kelly had also garnered the position of Brooklyn Borough historian. On his insistence, the old timbers were removed from the aquarium to the Museum of the City of New York, and saved for posterity.

When the Port of New York Authority released plans for the erection of a World Trade Center to be located in lower Manhattan, Kelly saw another opportunity to exhume the historic artifact, but once again he was disappointed. Today, the ship still lies yards away from the monolithic-styled structures, and only feet away from the rumbling of the I.R.T. number 1 train.

SEAL OF KINGS COUNTY. *This seal shows the original boundaries of Gravesend, as well as the five other towns in Brooklyn.*

2. FOUNDING AND SETTLEMENT

The Dutch West India Company, formed in 1621, petitioned for a trading charter in New Netherland, and on June 3, 1621, the charter was granted. It was not, however, until March 1624 that a group of nearly 30 families, for the most part Belgian Walloons, left Amsterdam, Holland, on the *Nieuw Nederlandt* for their journey across the Atlantic. In May 1624, they arrived in New York Bay. Director General Cornelus J. Mey served as the first governor of this new province. Mey was succeeded in 1625 by William Verhulst.

On May 4, 1626, Peter Minuit replaced Verhulst, and in so doing, the West India Company moved from its location at Fort Orange to Manhattan Island. Minuit, a Huguenot from Wesel, Prussia, has assured himself a place in history for his famed purchase of Manhattan Island from the Indians. He obtained the entire island for the merchandise value of 60 guilders, approximately $24. By requesting that families move to the island from Fort Orange and other adjoining areas, Minuit is credited with founding New Amsterdam, or today's Manhattan.

In Juet's log of the *Half Moon*'s voyage, he referred to Manhattan as "Manna-hata." A map printed in 1610 shows the island as Manahata and Manahatin. Even when the Dutch were firmly established on the island, they called it "the Manhattans," but many of the inhabitants still called it Manadoes, Manatus, Manhath, and even Mennadens. The origin of the word is still unclear, but many hold to the concept that it was the Indian word for "island" or "island of the hills." Minuit was recalled by the Dutch West India Company and replaced in 1632 by Governor Bastiaen Jansen Crol, who in turn transferred authority to Governor Wouter Van Twiller in 1633.

The formation of New Amsterdam served as the foundation for the future development of a town that was to embrace Brooklyn's maritime provinces of Coney Island and Sheepshead Bay, a town that would for the first time in the New World offer religious freedom to its inhabitants, a town that would have a "Master Plan"—a town named "Gravesend."

AVEBURY MANOR. Deborah (Dunch) Moody resided in this family home in Wiltshire, England, prior to her marriage to Sir Henry Moody.

Darkness had ended as the first rays of the rising sun raced across the lifting fog. The grass, still moist from the dew, muffled the footsteps of the midwife hurrying to the Dunch's home. Within moments of her arrival, the peaceful and serene atmosphere of the early morning was shattered by her one quick slap. The cries of the new-born female child brought tears to the proud father and mother who named her Deborah. Nearly 60 years after this event, Deborah would have her turn to serve as midwife to a town, which she herself would slap life into and name Gravesend.

She was named Deborah after her mother, who was the daughter of James Pikington, bishop of Durham, who was related to the Kingsmill family. Her father, Walter Dunch, the younger son of Sir William Dunch of Little Wittenham, married Mary Cromwell, daughter of Sir Henry Cromwell and aunt to "the Protector," Oliver Cromwell. Deborah's family was prominent among those who favored liberty of conscience and freedom of Parliaments. Her father was a member of Parliament during the reign of Queen Elizabeth I. The fact that her grandfather was a bishop helped mold her idea of the right to worship God according to conscience. The venerable bishop's influence, although he had passed on prior to the young Deborah's birth, deeply impressed her as a child and did much in forming her character. Being well educated, she was taught Latin and therefore both read and wrote it well. Her father died in 1594 at the age of 42. Deborah's mother remarried after a short period of mourning.

Deborah Dunch was born in the year 1586, having been baptized in London on April 3 at Saint Giles Cripplegate. She was born more than likely at Grays Inn in London. There is a possibility, however, that she might have been born at Avebury Manor in Wiltshire. According to the *Wiltshire Vistation Pedigrees*, 1623, Deborah Dunch and Henry Moody registered their marriage on November 30, 1605, at Saint Mary Aldermary in London. The ceremony actually took place on January 20, 1606, at the same Cripplegate parish church. Henry Moody from Garsdon, Wiltshire, England, was sired by Richard Moody and Christine, daughter of John Barwick of Wilcot. Henry was knighted and created a baronet on March 18, 1606, by King James. On February 7, 1607, Deborah gave birth to her first child, who was named after his father, Henry, and in 1608, her second child was born, a female they named Catherine. Catherine married John Snow of London at the age of 19 on February 7, 1627. Catherine, it seems, never came to the New World. Deborah and Henry spent most their time together at Garsdon Manor in Wiltshire.

After a marriage of 24 years, Sir Henry Moody died on April 23, 1629, leaving behind a widow with two children. With Sir Henry's death, his son, Henry Moody II, assumed his title as knight and baronet. Lady Moody vowed, after the passing of her husband, that she would never re-marry. She remained at Avebury Manor until she grew tired of the rural community. With a new desire to relocate, she sailed up the River Thames to London. Once in London, Deborah became

GARSDON MANOR. *This is the Moody family residence in Wiltshire, England, where Deborah and Henry Moody lived upon their marriage.*

interested in the various religious movements of the time. After several months had elapsed, the Court of the Star Chamber discovered that Lady Moody had exceeded her allowed time limit to remain outside of her community. She was then ordered to return home within 40 days. It was on April 21, 1639, that the court ordered that "Dame Deborah Mowdie, and the others, should return to their hereditaments in forty days, in the good example necessary to the poorer class."

As a result of this interference with her personal freedom, plus the displeasure of King Charles I at her religious tenets, Lady Moody gathered her skirts and boarded a small ship headed for New England. She left England from Gravesend in Kent County, with some followers, never to return. It appears that her son, Henry, later joined her in the New World.

Lady Moody arrived in the Massachusetts Bay Colony in April 1640. In Lynn, Massachusetts, she joined the Salem Church and became a follower of Roger Williams. According to Thomas Lechford, a local lawyer, "Lady Moody lives at Lynn but is of the Salem Church. She is a good lady but almost undone by buying Master Humphies' farm Swampscot." Lady Moody had purchased a home and 400 acres of land from John Humphrey on what today is Elmwood Road in Swampscott in Lynn, Massachusetts. The original deed to the land was lost, but a number of years later, Major William Hathorn, who was one of the appraisers, stated the following:

> about thirty yeares agoe when my Lady Moody first came ouer & mr Humfryes had received of her elevn hundred pounds, as they were both agreed, Capt Turner, Mr. Edward Tomlin & my self were chosen by them to value an estate that was prsented to us by mr Humfry, pt of which estate was the house & land in which he then lived cared Swampscott, we had an order delivered to us, made at new Towne, vy the Generall Court directing us to the bounds which weere by estimation, a mile from the sea side, & run to a great white oake, neere the Rock and soe to the Rockes upon the same line: the other farme on the north fell som yeares after into my hands, whoe knowing what wee had valued before, I sold to mablehead, & noe further to the southward, & from Rock to the spring, between Georg Farrs & Thomas Smithes.

In 1641, Lady Moody brought a writ of replevin against Francis Ingalls to recover a horse. But problems had only begun for her. In 1642, Lady Moody was indicted for not believing in infant baptism. Lady Moody and her followers were Anabaptists, or Mennonites, and therefore according to their faith, they did not believe that a child should be baptized at such a young age when he/she could not understand or know into what he/she was being baptized. The court proceedings in December 1642 reported that "Lady Deborah Moody, Mrs. King, and the wife of John Tillton were presented for houldinge that the baptising of Infants is noe ordinance of God."

Governor John Winthrop, first governor of the colony, described her in the following way:

> The Lady Moodye, a wise and anciently religious woman, being taken with the error of denying baptism to infants was dealt with by many of the elders and others, and was admonished by the church of Salem, whereof she was a member. But persisting still and to remove further trouble, she removed to the Dutch, against the advice of all her friends. Many others, infected with anabaptism removed thither also. She was after excommunicated.

Lady Moody was bold, relentless, and obstinate at times, living up to her heraldic coat of arms, which signifies the brave, the bold, the resolute, the gallant, and the courageous. One can picture Lady Moody as the Bella Abzag (a former United States congresswoman from New York City who was outspoken for women's rights) of the day, with her bonnet on and her voice upraised.

Lady Moody decided to leave New England for a clean, fresh start in New Amsterdam, where the Dutch would allow her to practice her faith. The Dutch had experienced persecution under Spanish domination, and finally in 1609, they received their independence. With similar experiences, Lady Moody renewed her hopes for a "promised land." She left her estate in Swampscott without selling it. She, however, rented it for about ten years to Daniel King, who was the husband of the aforementioned Mrs. King, who was also presented with her for denying the efficacy of infant baptism. In 1651, Sir Henry Moody, Lady Moody's son and lawyer, brought suit against King "for detaining a farme to the value of 500 li." Finally, King purchased the land from Lady Moody.

Many people left Lynn at about the same time that Lady Moody departed. The Massachusetts Records for 1643 reads as follows: "The Rev. Mr. Walton of Marblehead is for Long Island shortly there to set down with my Lady Moody, from under civill and church ward, among ye Dutch." A petition to the General Court in 1645 refers to this migration: "Those fewe able persons which were with and of us it's not unknowne how many of them have deserted us, as my Lady Moody."

Lady Moody left New England on a small vessel. She passed through Cape Cod; Newport, Providence, Rhode Island; New Haven (Qinnepiac), Connecticut; and passed down the sound to Anne Hutchinson's home and the home of John Throgmorton (Throg's Neck) through Hellgate and into New Amsterdam. It was at New Haven, Connecticut, that the concept for the town plan, consisting of four blocks, might have been conceived. New Haven had a similar layout for its town. After setting foot on the ground, Lady Moody headed for Director General Governor Willem Kieft. It was with Kieft that Lady Moody expressed her hopes and desires for a settlement. For a short while, Lady Moody and her followers lived in the colony opposite Blackwell's Island (Welfare Island), which today would be Sixteenth Street and York Avenue in Manhattan. While she

MURAL OF LADY MOODY. This mural, painted in 1948, depicts Lady Deborah Moody and Governor Willem Kieft looking over the land of Gravesend.

was in New Amsterdam, she met a number of people who were interested in joining her in creating a new home. One of those who joined her was Nicholas Stillwell.

After a rather short stay in New Amsterdam, Lady Moody and her followers moved to a tract of land on the southern and western most end of Long Island. Long Island was known at the time as Savanehachee. The French defined the meaning of this word as a "Sea-indented Savana." This new tract of land became Gravesend, named by Lady Moody after Gravesend, England.

Once she was settled, Lady Moody began to lay out the town and plan for its future expansion. Her plans were temporarily disrupted when Indian warriors attacked the small colony in 1643. On several occasions, Lady Moody and her followers fought the warring tribes, and on one particular occasion, the governor sent his troops to help the unprotected town. The violence grew to such an extent that Lady Moody and her band of citizens left Gravesend in 1643. They sought asylum at Nieuw Amersfoort, known also as Flatlands. There, they remained until 1645, when the Indian wars subsided, thus permitting them to return.

Life soon returned to normal for the settlers, and in a matter of months, Governor Kieft granted a charter to the town, signing it on December 19, 1645,

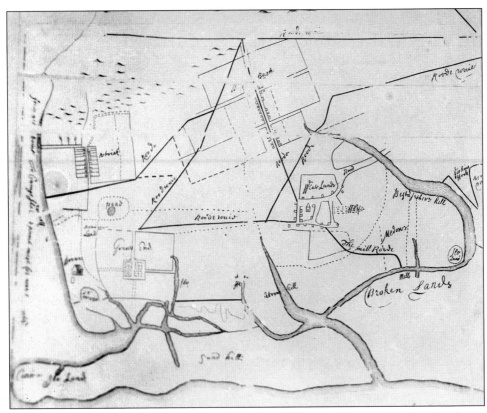

JAMES HUBBARD MAP OF GRAVESEND. This c. 1650s map is one of the first sketches to depict the boundaries and area of the town of Gravesend.

"unto the Honoured Lady Deborah Moody: Sir Henery Moody Barronett, Ensigne George Baxter: & Serieant James Hubbard."

This charter was unique in many ways. First, it was the only document of its kind in which a woman headed the list of patentees. Second, it provided for the establishment of an English town in the midst of a Dutch colony. Third, it, along with other Gravesend records and documents, were written in English as opposed to the other five towns of Brooklyn, whose records were written in Dutch. Fourth, it was the first document in the colony to grant any self-rule to an individual town. It provided, moreover, for three magistrates and an election of a "body politic," all of whom were subsequently elected by democratic ballot. The charter also permitted town meetings as were held in England. Fifth, it granted absolute freedom of conscience and the right to practice religious freedom "without magisterial or ministerial interference." This came even before the signing of the Flushing Remonstrance on December 27, 1657, which granted religious freedom in all of what was then America.

It may very well be said that Lady Moody was the first city-planner in the New World. She divided the village area of Gravesend into four perfect squares. She named the north street, Village Road North, and did the same for the South, East, and West, which has since been changed to Van Sicklen Street. The four squares were bisected by Gravesend Road, which later became Gravesend Avenue (now McDonald Avenue), and Gravesend Neck Road. A wooden palisade about 15 to 20 feet high was constructed around the perimeter of the four squares and afforded the settlers protection from the Indians and wild animals that roamed the area. Each of the quadrants was subdivided into ten plots. The houses bordered the streets, leaving within the center of each quadrant a common yard where the animals would be brought each evening from the open property outside the palisade for protection. Lady Moody then portioned the land outside the palisade like a pie to each of the settlers, who in turn farmed the triangular plots radiating from the village. If one were able to view this from the air at that time, the division of land would have resembled the spokes of a wheel.

Lady Moody was granted lots nine and ten in the northwest quadrant, called a "bowery." There, she built her home, which was the largest of the other homes constructed at the time of its completion in 1645. Her home still stands at 27 Gravesend Neck Road; however, many doubt that this home actually belonged to her. Charles A. Ditmas stated the following in the early 1900s: "It has been said that Lady Deborah Moody lived in this house. There is no foundation for that statement, either in fact or history. . . . Much that is interesting in regard to the title of this property will be discovered when the Gravesend records have been

LADY MOODY HOME. *This 1923 photograph shows a side view of the famous residence, a place where both Dutch governors Kieft and Stuyvesant sought Lady Moody's advice.*

finally gone over by the Commissioner of Records' experts." Years after this statement, Dr. James A. Kelly, the famed borough historian of Brooklyn, conducted a study of the home with the help of Clarence Nenning, the chief of the Map Room in the Office of the County Clerk, and Robert Rogers of the Home Title Company. They studied the overall structure of the residence, including the old wooden beams. Upon their investigation, the oldest wooden beams were dated to 1645. Since there is an unbroken chain of ownership of the property, there can be no doubt that the home is on the exact location of what was Lady Moody's property. Of course, the home has undergone so many changes over the centuries that it is very hard to believe that the home is over 350 years old.

The dormers that now cap the home were added toward the end of the nineteenth century, when an increase of population demanded such a change. The 14-by-14-foot kitchen, which was located on the right side of the home, is no longer there. Mrs. Isabelle Platt, who purchased the residence in the early 1900s, wrote an article about her home in the magazine *Country Life in America*. In the article, she mentions the work that was done refurbishing the home, including a new roof of cedar shingles and a steam furnace for heating. She described the home as follows:

> The house, which faces south, measures forty-two feet front by thirty-one feet deep, with a kitchen wing fourteen by fourteen feet. In the front there is a general living room, extending the full width of the building. At either end of this room are two great fireplaces, with large hearths measuring seventeen feet wide by eight feet deep of red Holland tiles eight by nine inches. The ceiling is beamed; these beams, the largest I have ever seen, still show the marks of the broadaxe, and are twelve by fourteen inches.

She also noted that many ancient coins were found throughout the structure and that a package of Colonial money along with two old pewter mugs and a brass tankard were found by the working men. The most interesting of the finds came when Mrs. Platt discovered documents in the attic of her home stating that Governors Kieft and Stuyvesant visited the home on numerous occasions. This discovery, along with the study by Dr. Kelly, validates the belief that this is the home of the founder of Gravesend, Lady Moody.

However, some continued to believe that her home was off to the north, outside the northeast quadrant where Village Road North meets Village Road East. This would seem rather absurd, for this would mean that the home stood outside of the palisade, which was, in effect, built to afford protection to the early settlers. This belief came into existence for the following reason. On the original Town Plan, which was drawn in 1645, the following is written above the northeast quadrant: "The land of Lady Moody." This naturally would lead one to think that it was here that her home stood. But to the left side or top of the northwest

LADY MOODY HOME. The Van Sicklen family is seen here in the 1870s posing in one of the oldest known photographs of the Lady Moody Home.

quadrant on the Town Plan, the same inscription, in the same handwriting, is written; obviously, the writer made an error and just simply rewrote the wording on the proper side.

Mrs. Grace E. McKeon once wrote in the *Brooklyn Eagle* that "The old house at 27 Neck Road was never the home of Lady Moody . . . a friend of mine, one of the best informed residents of old Gravesend, showed me the deeds of the historic house built at 27 Neck Road by Ferdinand Van Sicklen in the year 1709. Enough said A. Van Sicklen built the house." Or so she thought, for as was mentioned before, deeds can be traced back to the time when Sir Henry sold the home on May 11, 1659, to Jan Jansen Verryn up until the time when Nunzio Maisano purchased the home in June of 1955.

The chain of ownership for the home at 27 Gravesend Neck Road goes as follows. From Sir Henry, the home went to Jan Jansen Verryn, as was already mentioned. Verryn sold it to Ralph Cardall, whose widow married Thomas Baylie. Baylie died, and Mrs. Baylie married a third time, this time to Isaac Haselbury. Haselbury, together with Richard Gregory, purchased the site on February 11, 1689. In 1701, Haselbury sold it to Nicholas Stillwell. On January 9, 1702, the property was bought by Reynier Van Sicklen Jr., son of the first Fernande Van Sicklen, who arrived in New Amsterdam on the *Gilbert Beaver*. From Ferdinand Van Sicklen Jr., the property passed by a will dated June 25, 1737, to his son, Ferdinand, who married Maria Van Nuys. He left the property to his two sons, John and Abraham, and a daughter, Maria, who married Cornelius

Antonides. Both brothers divided the land and sold it afterwards in 1841 to Thomas Hicks, who sold it to William E. Platt in 1906. Years afterwards, the home was sold to Bert M. Coles, who sold the home to Mrs. Annie Anderson. During World War II, the Moody home was occupied by the Trapani Twins Post of the Veterans of Foreign Wars, so named for Charles and Frank Trapani, who grew up in the neighborhood. In June 1955, Nunzio Maisano purchased the home and within a matter of a few months spent over $6,000 modernizing it. Today, the home is owned by Maisano's son-in-law, Joseph Solmo.

Tales of ghosts and hauntings are often associated with old homes; the Lady Moody Home is no exception. In 1944, when Mrs. Annie Anderson lived in the home, many people thought she was the reincarnated Lady Moody. The following was taken from a May 17, 1944 article that appeared in the *World Telegram*:

> No, I don't think I am Lady Deborah, but I do believe she is near. I've sat alone in front of the fireplace here many a night and been afraid to turn around because of the footsteps I heard behind me. I think Lady Deborah's spirit is walking now because her home and mine has been looted and is going to be sold for taxes. . . . Some say Lady Moody never lived here. That isn't so. Before I moved into this place, I asked Mr. Stryker, the oldest man in Gravesend, where Lady Moody's house was. He said, "Walk up Neck Road; it's the Dutch house with the high hedge around it, opposite the old burying ground." . . . When Mr. Stryker was a boy old-timers used to recall that Lady Moody's ghost would never let her home be torn down. At the last minute, they said, somebody always turned up to save it.

From the way history has unfolded over the years with regard to the home, there may very well be some truth in that last sentence.

Some Gravesenders today believe that there are tunnels leading from Lady Moody's home to the Gravesend Cemetery and in other directions. This may have been true a number of years ago, but after careful inspection, there are no such tunnels. After modern construction of the streets, if there had been tunnels, they most certainly were destroyed.

When looking at the Moody home, which is also known as the Hicks-Platt home and the Van Sicklen home, one is looking at a structure that has undergone numerous changes. About 95 percent of the Moody home has been changed. At one point in its history, the house caught fire and a great portion of the home was destroyed, but yet it was repaired and restored.

Before Lady Moody's arrival to Gravesend, a variety of Indian tribes and villages occupied the town site. The French navigators referred to the Indians as "la gente canarde," or the "duck tribe of people." Other explorers corrupted the name into canarse, then into canarsier, canarsee, until the name emerged to today's word as Canarsie. The Canarsie Indians occupied King's County and various sections of Queen's County and Jamaica.

SEA GATE, 1920. The early Narriockh tribe once lived in a village here. Visible on the right across the filled-in ground is the lighthouse.

In Gravesend, there were Indian villages consisting of five tribes: the Narriockh occupied what is now known as Sea Gate; the Mannahanning was located between Cropsey Avenue and the Belt Parkway between Bay Forty-Sixth Street and Bay Fiftieth Street; the Massebackhun was located around Stillwell Avenue, where the Marlboro Houses are today; the Morpeesah's village stood between Ocean Parkway and Coney Island Avenue between the Belt Parkway and Avenue Y; and the Makeepaca stood on the site where the Sheepshead Bay and Nostrand Housing stands today.

It is interesting to note that each tribe had one chief as leader who was called a sachem. With this title, the chief could declare war, sign peace treaties, and preside over council fires. The Indians had a usufructuary concept of land, meaning they believed that no one could really own land. When the first European settlers gave them some gunpowder and sewan and had them sign a piece of paper, they thought that the white man wanted them to move on for awhile, knowing that they could return whenever they wanted. The Indians felt that the white man was giving them gifts, so why not move away for awhile. Unfortunately, they misunderstood the land philosophies and practices of European society, for they failed to realize that what they signed was a document selling their land. And so only when they returned did the Indians understand clearly what had happened, and thus the violent conflicts began. Time moved on as the Indians moved out of the area or assimilated themselves to the customs of the Dutch and the English.

In the year 1636, Andreas Hudden and Walpert Garratsin (Gerritsen) occupied land off what today would be Avenue V and Gerritsen Bay near Marine Park. This area was later to become part of the Town of Gravesend. Gysbert Op Dyck, who settled in New Amsterdam, obtained a patent for Conynerz Eylandt (Coney Island) in 1642.

Anthony Jansen Van Salee, who many claim was a Dutch-speaking former black slave, was granted after a number of years of waiting, a patent for a tract of land along Gravesend Bay, which lay partly in Gravesend and partly in the Town of New Utrecht. He had applied for this land in 1639, but the application was denied. On May 27, 1643, he was granted 200 acres. Director Willem Kieft had purchased the land from Penhawitz, who was the sachem of the Canarsie Indians. Van Salee was nicknamed the "Fez," from his having lived in Morocco, where he engaged in privateering against Spanish and Catholic ships. Robert Pennoyer followed Van Salee by obtaining a patent for land on November 30, 1645. His land stood where the Unionville and Ulmer Park sections of Gravesend were later located. Anthony Johnson also held title to land before Lady Moody. As time went on, the Town of Gravesend acquired these properties

Lady Moody was a woman of refinement. She had the largest collection of books in all of New Netherlands. Many of her books were written in English, Italian, and Latin. For a short time it seems that Lady Moody wanted to return to New England. A passage in a letter from John Endicott to Governor Winthrop, dated 1644 from Salem confirms this wish to return: "I desire that she may not have advice to return unless she will acknowledge her evil in opposing the churches, and leave her opinions behind her, for she is a dangerous woman." She never returned to New England, for this "dangerous woman" was not likely to "leave her opinions behind her." But what was so dangerous about a woman who in good conscience wanted to have the freedom to practice openly her own faith?

In 1653, Director General Peter Stuyvesant complained about the election of the magistrates of Gravesend by referring to the townspeople as "the people of Gravesend who elect libertines and anabaptists." It is very interesting to note that Europeans who were leaving their native countries because of religious persecution came to Gravesend to practice their faith without any fear.

According to local legend, one of the first Quaker meetings in the New World took place at the home of Lady Moody. Upon hearing that Quakers who had gone to New England were being persecuted in America, Reverend Robert Hodgson left England for Boston. After weeks at sea, a tempest raged and the small vessel was blown off course, landing in New Amsterdam. When word reached Lady Moody that Hodgson was in New Amsterdam, she immediately invited him and his followers to Gravesend. Gerard Croese, although considered an inaccurate Dutch historian, wrote about Lady Moody and the Quakers' visit of 1657 in the following manner: "There was at Gravesend a noble lady, the countess of Morden who turned Quaker. She gave the people of this Society the liberty of meeting in her house, but she managed it with such prudence and observance of time and place that she gave no offense to any stranger or person of any other religion than her own, and so she and her people remained free from all molestation and disturbance." Whether Lady Moody really turned Quaker is not actually known.

Her kindness to the Quakers may have been interpreted by Croese as conversion to Quakerism.

Although the Gravesend charter granted religious freedom to the people of the town, Governor Stuyvesant would not stand for such a liberal movement as the Quakers presented. He started a persecution campaign against the invading "heresy," proclaiming a law whereby any colonist who entertained a Quaker would be fined 50 pounds. Dominie Megapolensis, who was head of the provincial church, petitioned that Lady Moody be brought before the governor and consistory of the church for using "calumnious expressions against God's work and his servants." Lady Moody was not brought before the authorities; however, the Quakers left Gravesend and made their way to Flushing and Hempstead.

Stuyvesant constantly had his spies keeping a watchful eye on the citizens of Gravesend. He never knew for sure whether or not this English colony might someday wish to be governed by an English governor. On September 28, 1647, Stuyvesant submitted a proposition that stated the following:

> On the day before yesterday, I was informed by Mr. Harck, Sheriff of Flushing, that a certain Scotchman named Forrester had come there to Flushing with commission to take possession as Governor of Long Island and of all the Islands situate within five miles there abouts; that this Forrester had spent two nights at Heemsteede and one night at Flushing, with our vassals and subjects there, where he had exhibited his commission. He came here on his way to Gravesend and Amersfoort there to exhibit his commission to the English residing under our allegiance and the Company's lands, which were granted them by charter from their High Mightinesses, our Sovereigns. We have demanded his commission and order of this said new Governor, and asked by what authority he came within our limits? To which he gave for answer, that he came here to demand my commission and authority. Wherefore I had him taken into custody, and on the next day had him placed under arrest at the City Tavern at the Company's expense, and having obtained his commission found one with an old seal depending, but not signed with any name, and, besides, a power of attorney signed by the Parliment, and nothing more. The further question is, What shall be done with said pretended Governor? Thirdly, that the commissioner please to make a final disposition of the criminals in prison, particularly Picquet.

In 1655, according to the *New York Colonial Documents*, Lady Deborah Moody became the first white woman ever to cast a vote in what is now the United States. So far as the records show, only one other colonial woman, Mrs. Margaret Brent of Maryland (1648), ever "wanted" to vote. Woman suffrage was not permitted in any of the colonies so the Moody instance stands out as unique.

GRAZING IN THE 1920S. *This scene in Brooklyn's Crown Heights is similar to how the first settlers of Gravesend would have raised their livestock in the area.*

Prior to serving as the "Capital of the Amusement World," Coney Island served as a raising ground for Lady Moody's pigs. On one occasion, when the ship *Seven Stars* came into Gravesend Bay, the crew discovered a number of pumpkins growing and took 200 of them aboard ship. They also found some pigs, which they also took along with them. Later when they were told that the pigs belonged to Lady Moody, the crew purportedly stated that "If we had known that these pigs belonged to Lady Moody, we would not have touched a single one of them."

After many cold winters and warm summers had transpired on the beautiful lands of Gravesend, Lady Moody died sometime between November 4, 1658, and May 11, 1659. On May 11, 1659, the Town Record states that Sir Henry Moody sold the home of his deceased mother, Deborah Moody. Where is she buried? No one really knows. Around this period of time, many Gravesenders were purchasing land in Monmouth County, New Jersey. It is very possible that Lady Moody had purchased land there and even possibly died there or on her way there. The Town Records do not stipulate her death officially. They do not give a precise date nor anything to that effect. One can be sure that if she had died in Gravesend, she would have been given a large write-up in the Town Records. Since 1650, all deaths and marriages were recorded. Why no mention of the founder of the town? Or could there have been a mention of her in the Town Records? There are a number of pages of the Town Records that are missing and it may very well be that her death may have been recorded on one of those pages.

For a number of years many people believed Lady Moody was buried in the Gravesend Cemetery under an unmarked tombstone. After several years, the tombstone was uplifted and to the amazement of all appeared letters that did not correspond to those of Lady Moody. She is more than likely buried within the smaller section of the Gravesend Cemetery.

Sir Henry Moody remained in Gravesend for a short while until his departure for Virginia. *Hening's Statutes at Large*, a collection of the laws of Virginia from 1619 to 1792, states, "By Act of the General Assembly on October 12, 1660 it was ordered that Sir Henry Moody bee imploied in an embase by the right honourable the Governour to the Manados about affairs of the countrey shall have eleaven thousand pounds of tobacco out of the levie this yeare as a gratuity for his pains therein." Sir Henry Moody, it seems, was obliged to offer as security the verification of his father's knight's order given by King James when he became deeply involved in debt. He also owed a board bill at a little inn in New Amsterdam. Gone was the founder and her son. But never were they to be forgotten!

Town records often offer the reader a glimpse of the lifestyle of the people of the town. Gravesend's town records being written in English helps today's researchers to understand with ease and to learn how these simple town's people lived. All births, deaths, and marriages were recorded and documented in the town records. It is interesting to note that the records state that the landowners had to fence in their properties and if they did not build a "suitable" house upon the property that they would in fact forfeit their right to the land.

Town meetings were planned so that good communication amongst the settlers would exist. Meetings were called on the first Monday of every month between eight and nine a.m. It was at these meetings that problems between neighbors would be resolved.

John Tilton became Gravesend's first town clerk. He received from each inhabitant of the town one gilder, which was about 40¢. His job was difficult at times. He had to record the problems of feuds, stealings, and name calling by these early settlers. It sounds almost as if he served as a present-day court stenographer. The first "scoute" of the town was Sargeant James Hubbard, who was elected by the people on January 22, 1648, to maintain the laws of the town.

An intriguing case was that of Ralph Cardall versus Robert Pennere. This case took place on May 7, 1647. It appears that Mr. Cardall accused Mr. Pennere of stealing his tobacco. John Morrice, who served as a witness, stated that Mr. Pennere liked to trade tobacco with the Indians and when he needed more, went and took some out of Mr. Cardall's tobacco house.

Laws were established to protect the townspeople. Wild animals such as foxes and wolves presented a menace to their society. A law was established so that if anyone were to kill any of these beasts a reward of two gilders (80¢) was granted for a dead fox and three gilders ($1.25) for a dead wolf. Slander was a common occurrence among the townspeople, and people were accused of milking other people's cows and stealing other items that were dear to them.

Every town has its bad apple and Gravesend was without exception, for it had the notorious Thomas Aplegate. It appears that on January 8, 1651, he was accused of saying that "the governor takes bribes." Witnesses came forward and stated that he did indeed say this about the governor. The court felt that Mr. Aplegate should have his tongue bored through with a red-hot iron and that he should make a public acknowledgment of his statement. However, upon his confessing to the offense, the court chose to fine him 12 gilders ($4.80).

Intemperance and slander were not to be tolerated in the town. Not more than a pint of liquor was sold to a white man at a time and God help the person if caught selling the "laughing water" to the Indians. Disrespect for the Sabbath, theft, and refusal to pay one's debts were also punishable as was evident by many of the passages. Excessive drinking, rioting, horse racing, hunting, and ball-playing nine-pins on Sundays were considered disrespectful acts to God, and therefore fines were levied starting at ten shillings.

With modern telephones, computers, and other multi-media communications, today's generations are able to keep in touch with one another. But the early settlers of Gravesend had to rely on a drum beat or the sound of a horn that would summon them to meetings, church services, etc.

On May 7, 1654, Coney Island was purchased from the Indians by the people of the Town of Gravesend. The town paid "fifteene fathom of sewan [sea shells used for money], two gunns and three pounds of powder." The purchase of Coney Island was worth about $15. In that same year, Nicholas Stillwell, with 40 men, resisted an attack by the Indians at the home of Lady Moody. In 1655, hostilities broke out again, and 67 white settlers in Staten Island were killed while the Indians crossed Gravesend Bay headed for Gravesend.

THE FUTURE OF CONEY ISLAND. From its humble purchase of roughly $15, Coney Island developed into a world-class resort area, as seen in this 1922 photograph of the boardwalk.

THE FORMER GRAVESEND DUTCH REFORMED CHURCH. The church and its Sunday school building (at left) is seen here c. 1890.

On March 18, 1655, the Reverend John Megapolensis of New Amsterdam wrote the following to the Classis of Amsterdam:

> God has led Dominie Johannes Polhemus from Brazil over the Carribbean Island to a village called Midwout, which is somewhat the Meditullium of the other villages, to wit: Breuckelen, Amersfort and Gravesend. There he has preached for the accommodation of the inhabitants on Sundays during the winter season.

This passage indicates that while Lady Moody was still alive, not only did the Quakers preach at Gravesend, but the Dutch Reformed Church was starting to plant its seeds.

On January 13, 1657, a petition of the Magistrates of Amersfort noted the following:

> In order to raise the three hundred florins in the easiest way [needed to make up their quota of said amount] we have assessed the property of each person, conscientiously and to the best of our knowledge, here below given in detail, which, with what some parties from Gravesend have voluntarily offered to contribute, will make up a sum of three hundred florins.

In 1660, a formal petition was drawn up by the inhabitants of Gravesend to the director-general and council of New Amsterdam calling for the appointment of a preacher for the town. Nothing was heard until after the British occupied New Amsterdam. The first church services for the Dutch Reformed Church in Gravesend took place in the Sessions House, which was the first building used for court purposes. This Sessions House, or courthouse, was the county seat used by what was later to become King's County, Newtown, and Staten Island. Gravesend was honored to hold the county seat until 1685, when a law was passed moving the county seat to Flatbush. The Sessions House was completed in 1667 and was shared with the Dutch Reformed Church until it moved. During the period from 1685 to 1705, not much is known about the Dutch Reformed Church in Gravesend. In 1701, when Wilhelmus Lupardus died, all the churches in King's County were without a pastor, for he was the sole minister who served the county. Gravesend shared pastors with the Dutch Town of New Utrecht beginning in the year 1715. Bernadus Ver Bryck was pastor of the Gravesend Dutch Reformed Church until 1749, when he was removed to North Branch, New Jersey.

Since 1667, the old Sessions House, stood on the northwest corner of what is now McDonald Avenue and Gravesend Neck Road. It had become dilapidated and therefore was demolished in 1760.

In 1762, the Reverend Martinus Schoonmaker helped revitalize the Dutch Reformed Church in Gravesend. The first Gravesend Dutch Reformed Church

DUTCH REFORMED CHURCH. A group of patriotic female marchers walk past the church during the Anniversary Day Parade c. 1898.

32

was built upon the same site as the old Sessions House, where the first services took place. This building faced south as does the Lady Moody Home today. It had a double-pitched roof and double doors at the entrance and was painted brown, both within and without the structure, with four windows of small panes, of upper and lower sash, on either side. There were two strong pillars, each about 15 feet from the end, supporting the roof. A gallery for young men ran across the south end of the church; under this were the quarters reserved for the black congregation of the church. The pulpit, at the church's north end, was a plain octagon coop, reached by a spiral stairway and perched upon a hole. The sides of the church were shingled and the inside sealed with boards. Surmounted on the top of the church was a belfry with a bell weighing over 80 pounds. Above the belfry stood a weathercock. There was no heating in the building except for the foot-stove, which housewives brought along with them from home.

This new house of worship opened for services on July 25, 1762. After a short while, Schoonmaker became the pastor of the churches of Harlem and Gravesend, taking up his residence in Harlem and traveling to Gravesend on horseback for services.

After a number of years, the church fell into deterioration. On November 13, 1832, a meeting of the consistory was called, and a committee consisting of Garret Stryker, Nicholas S. Williamson, and Samuel I. Garretson met to take up the matter of building a new church. Land behind the old church site was purchased from Cornelius I. Emmons for $250. The new site, an irregular lot, measured 65 feet by 146 feet by 113 feet by 104 feet, westerly along the old church lot 43 feet then southerly 48 feet to the place of beginning. The church itself measured 45 wide by 62 feet long. The new church was opened on January 5, 1834, on Gravesend Avenue (McDonald Avenue) facing east.

As the years passed, the railroad was built on Gravesend Avenue and many of the parishioners going to church were often hurt while crossing the tracks. Services were often interrupted by the loud clanging of Culver's railroad trains. In 1892, the congregation wanted to build a new church away from the noise and danger of the passing trains. Land was purchased for $6,000 on Gravesend Neck Road near East First Street. The contract of sale was signed on December 22, 1892, and on January 16, 1893, the deed was given to the principals in the transaction.

Peter Van Note performed the carpentry work on the new church, while Benville Schweimler did the masonry work at a cost of $22,750. The building was to be of washed brick with terra-cotta trimmings. The bids for the new structure were opened on August 4, 1893, and ground was broken on August 9, 1893, the pastor, Reverend Gardner, taking out the first shovelful of earth at eight o'clock in the morning.

On October 8, 1893, the cornerstone from the previous church was re-laid, with addresses by Doctors Brush and Wells and the Reverend J.S. Gardner. The completion of the church and its dedication took place on October 28, 1894. The Reverend Dr. Farrar of the Seventh Avenue Church in Brooklyn preached the

DUTCH REFORMED CHURCH. This photograph shows the former Gravesend Dutch Reformed Church, located at East First Street and Gravesend Neck Road, as it appeared in the early 1970s.

first sermon. The first service held in the new church was with the Executive Committee of the Young People's Society of Christian Endeavor, held on June 8, 1894, when the church was still unfinished. Pews for the church were a gift of the Christian Endeavor Society while the carpets were given by the Ladies' Aid Society of the church. The parsonage was erected and completed on August 25, 1901, at a cost of $4,550. This lovely, Gothic house of prayer can still be seen on Gravesend Neck Road and East First Street. It is today the Trinity Tabernacle Church of Gravesend.

On the morning of August 20, 1664, the British vessel *Guerney*, commanded by Colonel Richard Nicolls, entered Gravesend Bay and anchored into the upper bay area. Nicolls demanded that Governor Stuyvesant surrender New Netherlands to him. Nicolls came to New Netherlands to claim the territory in the name of King Charles II of England for the Duke of York, who was the king's brother. Stuyvesant, who was taken by surprise, had no choice but to surrender and sign the capitulation on September 8, 1664. And so New Amsterdam became New York. The Dutch, therefore, were no longer in command.

Gravesend had no choice but to adhere to this new government. Governor Nicolls ruled New York from 1664 to 1668. During that time, he issued a confirmatory patent to Gravesend on August 13, 1668, as did his successor Governor Francis Lovelace on July 1, 1670. These patents, or charters, simply confirmed all rights and privileges that were granted to the inhabitants in the original patent of December 19, 1645.

In the late seventeenth century, Gravesend seemed to have had problems dealing with its boundaries and the certain rights that went with them. The oldest and longest court case on record dealt with the boundary fight between the Town of Gravesend and the Town of New Utrecht over the catching, packing, and selling of fish.

On May 24, 1687, trouble began concerning the boundary between Gravesend and Flatbush:

> A protest of James Hubbard pattentee of Gravesend in ye behalf of him selfe & ye Inhabbitants of Gravesend. Maye ye 24th Anno 1687.
>
> Whereas in ye dayes of ye former Governours Coronell Richard Nicolls, & Coronell Francis Lovelace, his Mates Governour, Charles ye Second, King of England &c There were certaine pattents given for the, to the Respective Townes, as by there pattents maye appeare bounded, & adjaceing for ye good Subisitance of ye Respectives & Is now presumed by Some of ye Flattbush, to take libbertie to them selves, within our pattent of Gravesend to molest & truble us, within our Said Limmitts of pattent And there stete fore doe heareby forewarne & for bidd, Oakah Johnson, of ye Flattbush, or anye other of ye people or Inhabbitant of ye Respective Townes, to forbeare ye erecting or buildeing within our said pattent: & as hath been to Such Inhabbitants formerlie.

FLATBUSH, 1920. The Town of Gravesend had boundary disputes with the Town of Flatbush dating back to the late 1600s.

On November 29, 1683, an act conceived by Governor Thomas Dongan created the County of King's, which included Gravesend (the English town) and the five Dutch towns of Boshwych (Bushwick), Breukelen (Brooklyn), Nienw Amersfoort (Flatlands), Midwout (Flatbush), and Nieuw Utrecht (New Utrecht).

On September 10, 1686, Governor Thomas Dongan signed the last patent for Gravesend. With this final patent, the town of Gravesend comprised such areas that were once known as and/or are known today as Coney Island, Bensonhurst (named after Egbert Benson, who was a large landholder in Gravesend during the nineteenth century), Unionville, Ulmer Park (an area of Gravesend known for its dancing pavilion and summer picnic grounds), South Greenfield, Brighton Beach (named for the British sea resort of Brighton), Manhattan Beach, Pelican Beach, Plumb Beach, Marlboro, Sea Gate, and Sheepshead Bay (named supposedly by Benjamin Freeman after the sheepshead, a fish that lived in abundance off the bay).

The boundary for Gravesend was as follows: Its vertex (north side) was at Foster Avenue and East Seventeenth Street. The western boundary was somewhat disputed, so there are two boundary lines to be considered. The controversial border ran from Foster Avenue and East Seventeenth Street down to Twentieth Avenue and Gravesend Bay; the more accepted boundary line ran through Bay Parkway to Seventy-Eighth Street then south to Bay Thirty-Seventh Street and Gravesend Bay. The east boundary extended down Avenue L on East Seventeenth Street, where it swung over to Olean Street and ran southwest to Fillmore Avenue and Madison Place at the beginning of Marine Park and at the head of what was Stroom Kill, today called Gerritsen Bay. The southern boundary for the town was the shoreline of the Atlantic Ocean.

New Utrecht, 1924. This view shows Gravesend (McDonald Avenue) looking south from Eighteenth Avenue, near one of the patent lines between Gravesend and New Utrecht.

3. Evolution through Revolution

The colonial period sowed the seed for the growth of the Town of Gravesend. In October 1706, a town landing was built at Gravesend Beach, which stood at the foot of the Old Mill Road near Bay Forty-Ninth Street. With this new landing, the people of the town were able to travel by boat to Manhattan Island, much as people do today by subway for store shopping.

On April 8, 1728, a deed was signed that permitted the purchase of a small piece of land for the use of what was to be the first public school in the entire Town of Gravesend. This piece of land, 1 acre in extent, was located on the southeast corner of Gravesend Neck Road and McDonald Avenue. The deed was given by Jacobus Emans and was signed, sealed, and delivered in the presence of Samuel Hubbard and Aaron Emans. The deed describes the property as "one house and two garden spotts," and is given to "the freeholders and inhabitants of Gravesend, whose names are signed upon the back side hereof, to be used and employed to the use of a school by the owners thereof at all times forever hereafter, and for no other use or employment whatsoever."

This school accommodated the town for nearly 60 years when, however, in 1788 a new and much larger building was erected upon the same site. The school was a small, one-story wooden structure that measured 25 feet by 35 feet. The building was turned into the town hall in 1838 after a new school site was found.

The first road to Coney Island was started in 1734, while in 1763, another road was laid out along the north side of the middle division of Coney Island. By 1738, the population of the town had reached an overwhelming 268. The year 1754 marked the first recorded mention of the town supervisor, who was at the time the miller Samuel Gerritsen. The town supervisor functioned as a mayor of a town.

Gravesend played its fatal role in the Battle of Brooklyn, also known as the Battle of Long Island, exactly 49 days after the signing of the Declaration of Independence. On August 22, 1776, Admiral Lord Richard Howe and General Sir

William Howe, along with Generals Henry Clinton and Charles Cornwallis, landed with 20,000 troops and 400 ships at Gravesend Bay. General William Howe had encamped on Staten Island in the days before the Fourth of July, building up troops and supplies in preparation for the inevitable struggle with the Continental Army, headed by General George Washington.

The night before the August 22 landing brought with it a violent thunderstorm, which only added to the distress of Washington's soldiers. Within the ranks of the Continental Army, Captain Van Wyck and two lieutenants of General McDougall's regiment and a Connecticut soldier were killed by lightning. Washington, knowing of the British landing, stated the following in a letter dated August 20, 1776: "Nor will it be possible to prevent their landing on the island, as its great extent affords a variety of places favorable for that purpose, and the whole of our works on it are at the end opposite to the city. However, we shall attempt to harass them as much as possible, which will be all that we can do."

The British landed at Gravesend and at New Utrecht at the site of De Nyse Ferry, presently known as Fort Hamilton. The frigates *Phoenix*, *Greyhound*, and *Rose*, along with the bombketches (a type of naval vessel) *Thunder* and *Carcass*, moved slowly into the bay while Sir George Collier placed the *Rainbow* within the Narrows, opposite De Nyse Ferry.

THE BATTLE OF LONG ISLAND. *This memorial tablet stood on the side of the building at Fifth Avenue and Third Street in Brooklyn.*

SITE OF THE OLD STONE HOUSE. Seen here in 1922, this is the original location of the historic Cortelyou House, where over 250 Continental soldiers were killed by British troops under Lord Cornwallis.

First to storm the beaches were Count Colonel Emil Kurt von Donop's corps of chasseurs and Hessian grenadiers, with 40 pieces of cannon, and Lord Charles Cornwallis with the reserve, 2 battalions of light infantry, and 6 field pieces. Upon landing, they met with no resistance. Leading the array were the Redcoats of the British 17th Regiment of Light Dragoons. Behind them, following in order, were the British Grenadiers, British Artillery, and a column of German Hessians. They marched up De Bruynne's Lane (Twenty-First Avenue) and then on to the King's Highway, named by the British in 1704 for the King of England. While on King's Highway, a detachment of soldiers camped on the property of Joost Stillwell, the northwest corner of King's Highway and West First Street.

On August 25, 1776, an additional 5,000 troops of Hessians hired by the British and under the command of General Leopold Philip de Heister landed with two Hessian brigades. They also came over from Staten Island, only this time on flatboats. Baron Wilhelm von Knyphausen was second in command to de Heister. General Washington, General Charles Lee, and General Nathaniel Greene, along with Lord William Alexander Stirling and General John Sullivan, were some of the officers serving on the American side.

The Battle of Brooklyn reached its climax between August 27 and 29, 1776. The Old Stone House was taken over by General Cornwallis while General de Heister captured General Sullivan in Flatbush. General Washington, who was

WYCKOFF-BENNETT HOMESTEAD. Located on King's Highway and East Twenty-Second Street, this home, built prior to 1766, was occupied by Hessian officers during the American Revolution. The residence is listed as a New York City Landmark.

stationed in the Fulton Street area of Brooklyn, near where Borough Hall is located today, decided to leave Brooklyn before the British totally annihilated the American army. On the evening of August 29, 1776, Washington and his men boarded rowboats and under heavy fog left Brooklyn at the base of where the Brooklyn Bridge stands today. Had Washington not left Brooklyn with his 9,000 men, Americans today might be speaking with a British accent.

The British and Hessians continued their march up King's Highway on their way to Flatbush. The soldiers seized the Wyckoff-Bennet Homestead, which is located at 1669 East Twenty-Second Street, and used it as an encampment. In the late 1890s the Wood Harmon Company turned the land into an allotment. Streets were put through and the house, which faced south, was turned to face west. Today, the Wyckoff-Bennett Homestead is a New York City Landmark. This homestead, one of the few remaining Dutch Colonial farmhouses, was built by Henry and Abraham Wyckoff prior to 1766, and up until 1835, was owned by Henry and Abraham Wyckoff, who sold the home and property to Cornelius W. Bennett. The residence was owned up until recently by the Reverend and Mrs. Frank Curtis Williams. Mrs. Williams, who was the well-known Brooklyn poet Gertrude Ryder Bennett, maintained the home with great care and affection.

The two original, thick bluish-green windows, called bull's eyes, through which light filters into the hall, are still part of the front door of the home. The date 1766 was cut into a beam in the old barn, which has since been demolished. Two carefully preserved 4-by-7–inch window panes with the inscriptions

"Toepfer Capt. of Regt. de Ditfurth" and "MBach Lieutenant v. Hessen Hanau Artilerie" are the remaining legacies that the Hessians left. The Bennett Homestead originally occupied all the land from King's Highway to Avenue U and from Ocean to Bedford Avenues.

Nearby on Gravesend Neck Road across from Homecrest Avenue stood the home of Stephen J. Voorhees, who fought for the Continental Army as a member of the King's County Militia. One day after losing his way back to the encampment, he returned home to his wife, Phebe. While he was home, a Hessian soldier entered his residence and tried to drive off their cow, which was the only cow permitted alive in King's County. General Washington had ordered the harvested grain of the county's farmers to be stacked in the fields ready to be burned and their cattle to be driven beyond the expected lines of battle so that the enemy soldiers would not take advantage of them. Phebe, however, having recently given birth, needed milk for her child and therefore was permitted to keep a cow indoors. When Stephen saw that the Hessian was taking the cow, a fight ensued and Stephen killed the Hessian. For fear that the other Hessians would soon enough find out, he buried him in the cellar of the home.

Throughout the Revolution, the Lady Moody Home was temporarily used as a hospital for the wounded and a morgue for the dead. The militia of men who served on the American side from the Town of Gravesend are listed as follows:

LADY MOODY HOME. Seen here in 1910, the Lady Moody Home was used as a hospital during the American Revolution.

JANE STILLWELL HOUSE. This is a view of the Stillwell residence with the Gravesend Cemetery in the foreground. This cemetery is the final resting place for many local patriots.

Rutgert Van Brunt (colonel and member of the Provincial Congress), Rem Williamson (captain), Joost Stillwell (captain), Henry Wyckoff (first lieutenant, second regiment of Minutemen), Samuel Hubbard (first lieutenant), Garret Williamson (second lieutenant), and John Lane (ensign). Other patriots included Nicholas Stillwell, Rutgert Stillwell, Barnardus Ryder, Peter Williamson, Stephen Donly, and John Voorhees. All of these men played an active role in helping to preserve their freedom, and today they lie at rest in their ancestral land at the Gravesend Cemetery.

While the British occupied King's County, the inhabitants of Gravesend were embittered by the lawless Tories, or "plunderers," who often took the few morsels of food that they had. On one occasion, Court Lake, while walking to the old mill, took sight of an English soldier coming out of the mill carrying a bag of meal, which he naturally presumed was being stolen. While trying to stop him, an altercation ensued and they both found themselves on the ground fighting. The soldier tried to knife Lake's chest, but Lake, getting on his feet, seized the soldier's gun, which had fallen, and shot him. Lake then told the nearest neighbor, a Mr. Turnbull, and they both took the wounded soldier by wagon to his camp within the British lines.

Among the Town Records appear two old papers, one of which is dated 1778 and reads as follows: "A return of the officers and an exact Acct. of what every Inhabitant of Gravesend has against each officer, for his Board at six shillings N.Y. currency, and weeks from the time they were Billited until the 31 day of March 1778, inclusive." This document gives the name of each officer, his rank, time billeted, and the name of the inhabitant where quartered. It mentions for example, the amount of time spent at the quarters and the amount due. Eighty-eight officers, in rank from captain to ensign, and the names of 30 hosts are recorded in this document, which was signed by Captain Joost Stillwell. Many of the officers were charged with over one year's board.

Another document dated 1782 reads in the following manner: "A list of the money due the Inhabitants of the Township of Gravesend for the Boarding of Continentals and other officers, Prisoners, and some friends, as well hereunto appear by the following accounts. Gravesend, July 13, 1782." The boards of these officers eventually were paid by the state when in August 1790, Congress voted $38,000 "towards payment of persons in King's County for subsisting American prisoners during the late war."

As the rebuilding and repairing of the many homesteads of Gravesend continued, the people were once again orienting themselves to the peace and quiet

THE ELIAS HUBBARD RYDER HOME, 1929. Seen here at its original location on East Twenty-Ninth Street, the residence was later moved and is listed as both a New York City Landmark and historic place on the National Register.

of the ordinary chores of life. Many Hessian soldiers remained in Gravesend after the war ended and married American women, pledging allegiance to this new offspring that they had at one time tried to abort.

A proud and joyous day occurred with the arrival of President George Washington to the Town of Gravesend. According to his private diary, while on his general tour of inspection throughout Long Island, President Washington decided to visit the town. On Tuesday, October 20, 1789, President Washington stopped in the center of the town square, which today is the intersection of Gravesend Neck Road and McDonald Avenue, and visited the town school, which was later to become the town hall.

Many hearts were overcome with joy and emotion as he stood and shook the hands of the citizens. Court Lake was one of those fortunate enough to shake his hand. Many claim that Washington slept the night at the Lady Moody Home. This is very unlikely since there is no mention of this in his diary. He might have had, however, tea or some other refreshment at the home. The citizens of the town were mesmerized by that fraction-of-a-second handshake, and it would later have them enraptured re-telling the story perhaps on a cold, cozy, and snowy night beside the fireplace to their children, who would pass it on to their children and their children's children.

Gravesend remained a farming community, and changes manifested very slowly. Intermarriage among the English, Dutch, German, and Irish took place often, and as the year 1790 neared, the town's population reached 426 citizens.

THE SAMUEL HUBBARD HOME. *Samuel Hubbard served with the local militia during the American Revolution. The residence, located at 2138 McDonald Avenue, was built c. 1750.*

4. Gravesend Develops into a Resort Area

The 1800s were the years of growth and development for the town of Gravesend. Hotels, buildings, schools, amusements, and transportation of all kinds were established in this area. The turn of the century renewed the conflict between the Town of Gravesend and the Town of New Utrecht over the western boundary. Even until today, this particular case is the country's longest recorded court case, having lasted over 300 years. The Gravesenders fought the people of New Utrecht, and vice versa, over the right to fish at a certain area that both claimed to be their property. Since fishing was of great value to each community, one can see why everyone got upset over this situation.

In 1789, the Town of Gravesend called upon Aaron Burr, the renowned lawyer who was later to kill Alexander Hamilton in a duel on July 11, 1804, at Weehawken, New Jersey. He defended the Town of Gravesend in the Supreme Court at Flatbush, but not much good ever came of it, for the case was never truly adjudicated. By 1898, when the City of Brooklyn became part of Greater New York, there was no more need to continue with the court case since the land now belonged to one big, "happy" family.

The population of the town at the turn of the eighteenth century reached 489. The renewed conflict with the British in 1812 brought many men of Gravesend out of the farms and into combat. The following are some of the men from Gravesend who participated in that war: Richard Stillwell, Rutgert Stillwell, Nicholas Stillwell, Rutgert Stillwell II, Isaac Van Dyck, Henry Van Dyck, Garret Williamson, John Donly, Rem Van Cleef, Court Lake, Evert Stellenwerf, Hendrick Van Cleef, and Stephen Ryder.

Coney Island, which played an important role in the past century, had undergone a number of monsoon-like storms throughout its many years. Christmas Eve, 1811, brought with it an overwhelming deluge as did New Year's Day, 1839, when a phenomenal tempest washed away half of the island. Many ships were destroyed in both storms, leaving remnants on the shores of the beach.

THE JANE STILLWELL HOUSE OR C. LAKE HOUSE. This historic home was built c. 1800 on the east side of Van Sicklen Street, where Corso Court is now located.

Coney Island at one time was made up of three individual islands. The western-most end was called Coney; the center island, Pine; and the eastern-most island, Gysbert. As the years passed, these three islands were filled in and joined each other as seen today.

In 1834, the Town of Brooklyn became chartered as a city and gradually absorbed the towns of Bushwick (1855), New Lots (1886), Flatbush, New Utrecht, and Gravesend (1894), and finally Flatlands (1896). Williamsburg, which had been incorporated as a city in 1851, was annexed to the City of Brooklyn in 1855. Brooklyn, which means marshland, was named after Breuckelen, Holland, which was indeed a marshland.

Piracy had its part in the history of Gravesend. The crew of the rig *Vineyard* landed on November 29, 1830, in an open boat at Pelican Beach. The *Vineyard* had left New Orleans on November 9, 1830, headed for Philadelphia with a cargo of molasses, sugar, cotton, and Mexican coins worth nearly $54,000. Captain Thornby manned the ship with William Roberts, seamen Aaron Church, John Brownrigg, James Talbot, Henry Atwell, and the cabin boy Robert Dawes.

After a number of days out at sea, the black cook, Thomas Wansley, discovered that deep within the belly of the ship lay a silver treasure. He gathered together the crew and plans were made to kill the captain and mate. On the eve of November 23, the captain was standing on the deck of the ship while Dawes, the cabin boy, was steering. Arrangements had been made that when Dawes trimmed the binnacle light, Wansley would hit the captain on the head. And so it happened. The body of the dead captain was thrown overboard. Other members of the crew heard the commotion and a fight broke out atop the brig. William Roberts, the mate, was killed and also thrown into the ocean. The other crew members feared the mutinous sailors and so vowed to join them; the treasure was then divided.

Upon seeing Long Island, the pirates set fire to the *Vineyard* and headed for the lifeboats. There were two boats; one vessel held Gibbs, Brownrigg, Dawes, and Wansley with about $31,000 of the treasure. The other boat was occupied by Talbot, Church, and Atwell with the rest of the money. The ocean was rough and the gale wind overturned the second boat. Both crew and treasure went to the bottom. The other boat members, beholding this sight, panicked and began throwing the treasure overboard, unloading all but $5,000 worth. Upon landing at Pelican Beach, the four seamen buried the treasure with their oars.

After burying the treasure, the men met Nicholas S. Williams of Gravesend. They told him of the terrible shipwreck they had undergone. On hearing of their tragic event, Williams kindly showed them to the home of John Johnson. Johnson lived with his wife and his brother, William. The Johnsons treated the men with great kindness. They fed them and gave them drink. As payment, the men offered them a swordcane, a spyglass, and a silver watch.

While the others were asleep, Brownrigg confessed the actual bloody events to John Johnson. In the morning the sailors asked to go to a good hotel in Gravesend. John directed them to the local hotel, which Samuel Leonard ran.

At the same time that Brownrigg was telling the other men that he would no longer go on with them, the Johnsons were out on the beach digging up the treasure and finding a new place to hide it. Brownrigg told the entire story to the people in the hotel and before he was finished telling it, Wansley, headed into the woods. He was soon captured, and Justice Van Slyke issued warrants for the arrest of Brownrigg, Gibbs, and Dawes. Soon enough, they were incarcerated at Flatbush.

The Johnsons also got in trouble, for when Brownrigg took Justice Van Slyke to show him where the treasure was, it, of course, was no longer there. Suspicion fell on the Johnsons despite their sincere expression of innocence. Two large insurance companies sent agents to look over the Johnsons' home since they had shared coverage on the specie—the coins being shipped.

The Johnsons, meanwhile, decided that cutting in brother William was unnecessary, and they dug up the treasure once again, dividing it into parcels of $3,400 and $1,600. This time they marked the location of the treasure by tying knots in sedgegrass. William thought of the same idea but one night too late. Enraged at what his brother had done to him, he reported what had happened to the insurance men in New York City. They sued John, but it could not be proven that he had taken the treasure since the tides sweeping the beach had loosened the knots in the grass. After much searching, John was only able to find $3,400 worth of the treasure.

But what ever became of the pirates? Dawes, Wansley, and Gibbs, along with Brownrigg, were taken to Bridewell Prison in New York. All but Brownrigg were tried, convicted, and hanged on April 23, 1831, on Gibbert Island. When told that he was going to hang, Wansley replied, "I would like that better than if I was in

GERRITSEN'S PARK. This photograph was taken in November 1920 from a spot in today's Marine Park near Burnett Street. Gerritsen's Mill is visible in the distance.

the other boat, for I would not like to be drowned." Before dying, Gibbs confessed to having killed over 100 seamen, officers, and female passengers. His last words expressed the hope that "Christ will make my death as easy as if I had died on a downy pillow."

The New Year's storm of 1839 revealed the secret hiding place of the silver treasure since the dunes on the Pelican Beach were washed away. Fortuitous beachcomber Jacob Skidmore discovered a silvery shine emanating from the sand, and upon closer inspection, found silver dollars. Two of his neighbors, Willet Smith and Henry Brewer, started to fill their pockets and boots. Well, sure enough, the news spread and the "silver rush" was on. The next day, all businesses were closed in Gravesend and the entire town came to the beach looking for the "silver clams."

A similar incident but of less value occurred in 1877, when a schooner was swamped off Coney Island Point. The vessel carried on board a cargo of pineapples costing nearly $20,000. At that time, a pineapple was so exotic and rare that it was worth its weight in gold. When the townspeople found out that these precious pineapples were scattered all over the beach, sure enough, everything closed up and it was out to the beach again.

The Coney Island Road and Bridge Company, incorporated on March 22, 1823, by a legislative act, built Shell Road in 1824. John Terhune, then supervisor of the town, Van Brunt Magaw, and John S. Gerritsen were commissioned to do the work for a road 3 rods wide that would extend through the meadows between the property of James A. Williamson and Stephen H. Stillwell. Thousands of sea shells were used in the construction of this roadway, which included a bridge over the Coney Island Creek.

Additional capital stock was authorized by an amendment act in 1829 and a site procured from Court Van Sicklen on which the company erected the Coney Island House. The Shell Road was then known as the Coney Island Causeway, and it continued along Gravesend Avenue (McDonald Avenue), which was begun in 1838. In 1875, Gravesend Avenue (McDonald Avenue) was widened to 100 feet running to Coney Island Creek, which had to be crossed by a toll bridge. John Lefferts was the proprietor of Shell Road, and he collected the toll until 1876, when Andrew R. Culver bought him out and built his steam railroad along the road.

The opening of the Coney Island House in the 1840s signified the birth of Coney Island as a resort community since it was the first hotel to be opened on the island. The hotel was leased to Mr. Tooker for three years. In 1847, the property was sold half to John Terhune, who in the same year sold half of it to his brother, Abraham. John and Abraham later sold the property to Peter Lott.

The Coney Island House enjoyed many famous guests. Washington Irving visited the hotel with his niece in 1848, while Herman Melville visited in 1849. In July 1850, influential politicians Henry Clay and Daniel Webster spent some time at the hotel. Walt Whitman, who often enjoyed swimming naked off Coney's beach, and famous southern leader John C. Calhoun also signed their names to the registry. Other visitors included Sam Houston; William Macready, the English actor; Fitz-Greene Halleck, the poet; and James Gordon Bennett, publisher of the *New York Herald*.

John Wyckoff built the second hotel on the island, while Dr. Allan Clarke built the Oceanic Hotel, which stood near the Coney Island House and was destroyed by fire in 1854.

KING'S HIGHWAY, 1923. Roads played an important role in the commercial and social development of Gravesend and Coney Island during the nineteenth century.

RAVENHALL'S BATHING PAVILION. A large crowd of bathers are enjoying the September sun in 1919.

In 1844, two New Yorkers, Eddy and Hart, built a large circular platform of wood and topped it with a tent, which they named the "Pavilion." With this, the first amusement exhibit started on the island. These two men were later responsible for the building of the Wyckoff Hotel.

While the Civil War was going on, the island was still growing, adding many new facilities. Peter Ravenhall, a Brooklyn harness-maker, leased some land on the shore front from the Town of Gravesend and built a restaurant and bathing palace in 1863. Champagne luncheons and picnic-basket lunches were common enjoyments in and around Ravenhall's. Two years after the opening of Ravenhall's Restaurant, Peter Tilyou arrived and opened the Surf House, which served both as hotel and restaurant.

Early Coney Island stagecoach owners included James Cropery, A. Felter, John Carll, Patrick Breslin, Conklin Carll, and Thomas Cromwell. As early as 1847, a small sidewheel steamboat crossed the waters from Manhattan to the west end at Coney Island Point, which is today known as Sea Gate. By 1874, larger boats were introduced, and by 1880, the Iron Steamboat fleet of seven vessels commenced regular service to Coney.

The first railroad to reach the island was the Brooklyn Bath and Coney Island Railroad, also known as the "Dummy Line" since it ran so slow. It was later purchased by C. Godfrey Gunther. The Brooklyn, Flatbush, and Coney Island Railroad began operation in 1869, while in 1878, the Brooklyn and Brighton Beach Railroad was opened. Andrew Culver, who owned a number of small railroad lines, created the Prospect Park and Coney Island Railroad in 1876. This line ran on Gravesend Avenue (McDonald Avenue) and today is the route of New York City's "F" train. On March 16, 1919, the line became elevated from Ditmas Avenue to King's Highway. The el opened from King's Highway to Avenue X on May 10, 1919, and reached Stillwell Avenue by May 1, 1920. In 1875, the King's County Railroad Company ran with open cars.

Andrew Culver also brought to the island entrepreneur Thomas Cable, who built a 150-room hotel. Within one year's time, Culver carried over 1,000,000 passengers to and from Coney Island. He bought the Sawyer's Tower, which was later named the Iron Observatory, from Philadelphia's Centennial Exposition of 1876. Set up on the island in 1877, this iron structure stood over 300 feet high and had two steam-operated elevators and a telescopic eye on its top.

Ocean Parkway, which was at one time considered the "finest drive in America," got its start by J.S.T. Stranahan, who was the park commissioner of Brooklyn and headed the application to the legislature. An act passed May 11, 1869, amended on May 14, 1872, gave the necessary authority to "lay out, open,

Surf Avenue, c. 1900. The famous Iron Observatory was originally built for the Centennial Exposition of 1876 in Philadelphia and was later moved to Coney Island in 1877. (Courtesy the James A. Kelly Local Historical Studies Institute.)

OCEAN PARKWAY, 1922. This historic road, designed in 1866 and a registered New York Landmark as of January 28, 1975, is the "Champs Élysées" of Brooklyn.

and improve a public highway or avenue from Prospect Park, in the City of Brooklyn, towards Coney Island, to the lands of the Prospect Park Fair Grounds Association." Construction began in 1874 and was completed in 1875 ending at King's Highway. The extension from King's Highway to the Atlantic began in the spring of 1876. On November 18, 1884, the entire parkway, which ran 5.5 miles long, 70 feet wide, with two 25-foot roads on each side, opened from Brooklyn's "Arc De Triomphe," the Soldiers and Sailors Monument, to Coney Island. The roadway was completed at a cost of $1,000,000. This "Champs-Élysées," as the Gravesend Historical Society terms it today, was the scene of many family walks and impromptu bike-racing on any given Sunday afternoon in the golden years of the late nineteenth and early twentieth centuries. Today, Ocean Parkway is enjoyed by many pedestrians and bike riders. Ocean Avenue was completed in 1876, costing $315,000. This avenue was 100 feet wide and a little over 5 miles long. The Coney Island Plank Road, now known as Coney Island Avenue, was originally surveyed by the Honorable Tunis G. Bergen, who filed a map for it on October 12, 1849. In 1850, the road was completed and was 66 feet wide until 1872, when it too was widened to 100 feet. In its beginning, tollgates stood on each end of the roadway. Originally placed for horse riding, the planks on the road were removed in 1860 to accommodate horse cars. When the wagons were added, the ride became too rough as the wheels rode over them.

The New York and Manhattan Beach Railroad was begun in 1876 by Austin Corbin, the builder of Manhattan Beach. The New York Sea Beach Railroad, which is today the BMT's (Brooklyn and Manhattan Transit) train, was established in 1877. In 1913, plans drawn for the reconstruction of the line called for adding two more tracks and placing the stations and tracks below the surface of the sidewalk, yet leaving it exposed to the outdoors.

The first monorail system in the world was established in the Town of Gravesend by Eben Moody Boynton. The system ran during the summer of 1878, a distance of 3.7 miles from Locust Grove east through Gravesend to Brighton Beach. Due to bankruptcy, it was forced to close.

In 1843, the first official post office in Gravesend was opened. Located on Gravesend Avenue near Gravesend Neck Road for a time, this structure stood near the Dutch Reformed Church. Prior to 1842, all mail was sent to the Flatbush post office, requiring the people of Gravesend to travel to Flatbush to pick up their mail. Through the influence of Henry C. Murphy, who was then in Congress, the post office system came to Gravesend. Martin Schoonmaker served as the first postmaster. After serving in the position for over ten years, he resigned and Gilbert Hicks succeeded him on July 12, 1854. Other postmasters included John Bergen and Dr. R.L. Van Kleek, who took office on July 16, 1869. A new post office was later built in 1926 on Avenue U and West Fourth Street, where Eckerd's is today. The third structure of the Gravesend Branch Office is presently located on Avenue U and West Street. Another post office was established for a trial of one season at the Hotel Brighton. A third post office was also set up in the eastern part of the town at Sheepshead Bay. Today, there are ten post office branches located in what was the Town of Gravesend.

In 1868, a young man of 28 years arrived at Coney Island looking for some rest and enjoyment. While on the beach, William A. Engeman noticed that the salty sea air plus the clean, white sand produced a healthy atmosphere that he felt many

WILLIAM ENGEMAN.
This gentleman was an early developer and businessman of Brighton Beach.

MANHATTAN BEACH HOTEL, C. 1898. Austin Corbin constructed this magnificent hotel in 1877. (Courtesy the James A. Kelly Local Historical Studies Institute.)

would enjoy. Immediately, thoughts entered his head and he was off to see William H. Stillwell, the surveyor of Gravesend. At that time, the beachfront was part of the common lands of Gravesend, which were rented out on a yearly basis. Engeman had his eye on the middle division of the island, which lay just east of the center of the island. His main concern was how to purchase the land.

After winning Mr. Stillwell over by calling him "Judge," for indeed he was at one time a justice of the peace in Gravesend, Engeman took possession of several hundred acres of prime oceanfront property for $20,000. He then named the area Brighton Beach. Within a matter of four days, he built the earliest wooden pier on the beach. The old Iron Pier was later erected about 1878 and the New Pier was constructed on the site of Engeman's first pier.

The summer of 1873 brought to the beach a wealthy New York banker who had come to the beach with his wife and young son. He was Austin Corbin, according to the Oceanic Hotel's registry. By order of the family physician, Corbin came to the island for his son, who was ill.

While at the hotel, he began to enjoy the soft, warm breezes that the beach offered. He was so impressed that he introduced the slogan "Swept by Ocean Breezes" for his hotel, the Manhattan Beach, which was later to be constructed.

54

With a handful of ruffians and threats, Corbin was able to control the price that he intended to pay for the land upon which he wished to build. Corbin named his property, located at the eastern-most end of the island, Manhattan Beach. The majestic Manhattan Beach Hotel was opened on May 4, 1877, by President Ulysses S. Grant. Elegance and charm are the two words that could best describe this edifice of enjoyment and relaxation.

The Alexandra Fireworks Park was established in 1879 in the rear of the hotel. Henry Pain's Fireworks and Grand Pyro-Spectacle, delineating the war between Japan and China, thrilled many at the beach. Pain created many beautiful fire shows each evening (excepting Sunday) at 8 p.m. during the summer months. Pain's "Novelties and Surprises" included "Pompeii," "the Ninety and Nine Shells," "the Changing Star Bouquet of 100 Shells," "the Painite Volley of 500 Shells," and "the Chrysanthemum Garden of 250 Shells." The grounds of the Manhattan Beach Hotel would often be illuminated with prismatic lamps and Japanese lanterns, adding a golden touch to the dream-like atmosphere.

The Manhattan Beach Theatre, under manager B.D. Stevens, offered a variety of entertainment. Grand concerts were often played by Shannon's Twenty-Third Regiment Band; Thomas F. Shannon was director while Joseph Lacalle was his assistant. Lew Dockstader and his Minstrel Company performed, under the management of James H. Decker, such numbers as "Ida" and "Scandalous Eyes."

MANHATTAN BEACH HOTEL PROGRAM, 1903. This July program included such musical acts as Shannon's 23rd Regiment Band and Lew Dockstader and His Minstrel Company. (Courtesy the James A. Kelly Local Historical Studies Institute.)

The entertainment often commenced with the colossal spectacle, "the Hall of Fame," which was the largest and most costly stage ornamentation ever seen on American footlights at that time.

For other entertainment, there was also the Manhattan Beach Summer Opera House, where many arias were often heard. Grand spectacular transformation scenes included "Moonlight on the Mississippi," "The Sunny South," "The Colored Heaven," and "The Birth of the Sunflower." John Philip Sousa, accompanied by Isador Luckstone, highlighted the musical performances at Manhattan Beach by playing musical selections such as Verdi's overture, "Joan of Arc," and Liszt's "Second Hungarian Rhapsody." So in love with the mystical atmosphere of the beach was Sousa that he wrote "The Manhattan Beach March."

Edward E. Rice's Burlesquers, 70 in all, performed "1492" at the beach, and Rice brought to the beach his Circus Carnival. Anton Seral and his Metropolitan Opera House Orchestra played symphonies by the oceanfront. Manhattan Beach offered Gustave Kerkers Grand Orchestra of 50 artists and also Patrick Gilmore's Twenty-Second Regiment Band featuring Signor Raffaello on the trombone and Jules Levy on the cornet. The Manhattan Beach Hotel was host to the Union Club, the University Club, and the Coney Island Jockey Club. During this period of time when people had no radios, televisions, stereos, etc. for entertainment, live performances were in high demand.

By 1885, Diamond Jim (James Buchanan) Brady, a multi-millionaire who made his money from steel sales and horse racing, was seen spending two weeks of the year at the hotel. The hotel with its huge veranda offered him a great deal of enjoyment as he ate 12 to 15 lobsters in one sitting. In the morning, Brady would go swimming off the clear waters of the Atlantic. In the afternoon, there were

THE ORIENTAL HOTEL, C. 1900. This famous hotel was built in the late 1800s and demolished in 1916. (Courtesy the James A. Kelly Local Historical Studies Institute.)

THE BRIGHTON BEACH HOTEL, C. 1898. This hotel was also built in the late 1800s and demolished in 1924.

races at Coney Island Jockey Club. At night, he would often be seen with the lovely and attractive Lillian Russell. Both rode the gas-lit Feltman's Carousel, which today is located at Flushing Meadows–Corona Park. He was known as Diamond Jim since his tie clip, cuff links, and belt buckle, among other things, were made of diamonds.

Brady had a very unusual appetite. His breakfast included beefsteak, eggs, several chops, pancakes, fried potatoes, cornbread, muffins, and a huge pitcher of milk. The waiters at Manhattan Beach knew of his fondness for seafood, and so when they noticed that he was coming out of the water, they promptly scurried around to have a huge platter of chilled, freshly opened oysters ready by the time he would set foot on the porch.

In 1877, the Manhattan Beach Bathing Pavilion offered 117 bathhouses. The number of bathing houses grew gradually until finally in 1882, there were 2,350. Since changing on the beach was against the law, bathing houses were necessary. Manhattan Beach offered not only the Manhattan Beach Hotel, but also the Oriental Hotel, a larger luxury hotel that opened in 1880. Senator Thomas C. Platt, the Republican leader of New York State, made the Oriental his summer headquarters. The Oriental was often filled with the wealthy, while the Manhattan Beach entertained society people such as movie stars and other socialites.

The third largest hotel in Gravesend was the Brighton Beach Hotel, which opened in 1878. The Brighton Beach Hotel offered a summer home to the New York Club and the Bullion Club, among many others. Most of its guests were businessmen, politicians, and theatrical people. The hotel offered a park and Music Hall, which was under the management of Charles S. Breed. Famous performers such as Sophie Tucker, "the Mary Garden of Ragtime," singing "One of These Days," were often seen at the Music Hall. Louis Reinhard's Orchestra performed Irving Berlin's "They've Got Me Doing It Now" plus Jack Sidney and Billie Townley were other enjoyments at the Music Hall. Other memorable artists and troupes included Russell's Minstrel Comedians; Nellie V. Nichols, the Songstress Comedienne; the Five Sully Family in a travesty farce entitled *The Information Bureau*; Valerie Bergise, Brooklyn's favorite actress; Lillian Shaw, "the Dainty Singing Comedienne"; and Bert Fitzgibbon and Muller and Stanley in a parody of *Much Ado About Nothing*. Vaudeville had its day in the Town of Gravesend with all its shows and performances.

The Brighton Beach concerts were often put on by Admiral Neuendorf and his naval band. The Brighton Beach Park showed the Miller Brothers' famous 101 Ranch, with W.H. Kennedy as "arenic director," and this Wild West show was an actual recreation of cowboy life. The show featured a band of Sioux Indians, a bunch of cowboys from the Dogie Camp, a bunch of Oklahoma cowgirls, and Chief Bull Bear of the Cheyennes.

The New Brighton Theatre, "the Handsomest Seaside Theatre in the World," under the management of David Robinson, showcased Belle Hathaway and her Simian Playmates; the Kemps; the Ragtime Revellers; Charles Leonard Fletcher, America's "premier impersonator"; Maggie Cline, the Irish Queen; Latriska, the Human Doll; and Elfie Fay, "The Belle of Avenue A." All of these shows entertained those that were curious and brought smiles on their faces. Many of these entertainers worked these shows just so that they could get enough money to get by.

MUSIC HALL PROGRAM FOR BRIGHTON BEACH HOTEL, 1909. This musical program featured Irene Franklin as the "Queen of Vaudeville." (Courtesy the James A. Kelly Local Historical Studies Institute.)

BRIGHTON BEACH HOTEL. *This famous hotel was dramatically moved inland by rail to avoid the encroaching ocean's waters in 1888. (Courtesy the James A. Kelly Local Historical Studies Institute.)*

In 1906, the Manhattan Beach Hotel opened for the season on June 20 with T.F. Silleck of 289 Fourth Avenue as manager, while on June 28, the Oriental Hotel opened with Joseph P. Greeves as its manager. E. Clark King was the proprietor of the Brighton Beach Hotel, and he opened the door of the hotel on Thursday, June 14, 1906. The ocean air was considered at this time as being very therapeutic. Those that lived in Manhattan wanted to get away, relax, and breath in the fresh air. They also wanted a place that was close, so that they did not have to travel too far. The season ran from June to September. Coney Island, Brighton Beach, and Manhattan Beach provided this as a retreat for them.

Gilbert Hicks opened one of the first stores at Coney Island's "Point" in 1826. The "Point" was taken over in 1875 by Mike Norton, alias "Thunderbolt," when he built his Point Comfort House. He was called "Thunderbolt" because many a man who got into a fistfight with him described his punch as a thunderbolt. Norton's establishment, as time went on, became a notorious home of ill repute. As a matter of fact, the entire area became a "hang-out" for prostitutes, swindlers, and pickpockets. Norton was a captain in the Twenty-Fifth Regiment during the Civil War and was a political hack, being a member of both the board of aldermen and a state senator. The Irish-born politico had no problems when he wanted to set up his Point Comfort House. Boss Tweed of Tammany Hall was a good friend of his, and being such good friends, John McKane, the political tyrant of Gravesend, made sure that Boss Tweed's friends got good care.

CHARLES FELTMAN.
This early Coney Island entrepreneur is
remembered for his famous invention:
the hot dog.

Many famous men helped to make Coney Island the greatest amusement and resort area in the world. One of them was Charles Feltman, who was born at Verden in Hanover, Germany, in 1841 and helped to make famous the well-liked "hot dog." Cartoonist T.A. "Tad" Dorgan caricatured German figures as dachshund dogs shortly after the turn of the nineteenth century. Arriving on the island in 1871, Feltman is credited with adding the warm buns into which the "hot dogs" were placed. He rented a small shanty on the oceanfront from Martin Hook, to whom he paid $500 for the first year. At first, Feltman was turned down by Hook for the renting of the property. Feltman turned straight for Gravesend's Town Hall, where he met John McKane. McKane leased a large lot, adjoined to his own, to Feltman for $15 a year. The New Iron Pier was later to be built next to his property. Feltman, who is considered the first pioneer of Coney Island improvement, then built the Ocean Pavilion in West Brighton. Feltman catered mainly German-American food, and of course, no table was without a frosty stein of beer.

Charles Feltman worked at one time as a pie man. He had problems with John McKane when he first introduced the "hot dog." McKane actually believed that the meat used for "this hot dog" was that of a canine. After McKane's call for careful inspection of the meat proved him wrong, business began to boom, and Feltman began to expand. His restaurant and beer gardens were enjoyed by many as they listened to the music of the Sixth Regiment Band.

In the year 1880, Feltman installed one of Charles Loof's carousels in the beer gardens. This was the second carousel to be installed on the beach. The first stood at Lucy Vanderveer's Pavilion. Since business was doing so well, Feltman was in need of new help. A young man by the name of Nathan Handwerker, who had emigrated from Poland in 1912, began working for Feltman for a short while until he noticed that these "hot dogs" were selling like mad. "Why not go into business selling just hot dogs?" he thought to himself. With his life's savings of $300, Nathan set up his business on the corner of Stillwell and Surf Avenues, selling his frankfurters at a nickel a piece. Of course, Feltman did not like this and so there was competition. To increase his business, Nathan hired a group of college students to stand around his counters wearing white jackets with stethoscopes hanging out of their pockets eating his hot dogs. Word got out that the doctors from Coney Island Hospital were eating his "hot dogs," so they must be all right.

His "hot dog" was so beloved that in 1921 Sophie Tucker made a hit with the song, "Nathan, Nathan, Why You Waitin'?" Nathan finally dubbed his hitherto nameless stand, "Nathan's Hot Dogs." Since 1916, Nathan's Hot Dogs has served millions of hungry appetites and has since become the mecca for every aspiring New York politician. The 100,000,000th "hot dog" was sold on July 6, 1955. On March 24, 1974, at the age of 83, Nathan passed away.

By 1946, Feltman's Bavarian beer started losing its popularity, and so the business was sold to new owners, who subsequently went bankrupt in 1954.

THE BOARDWALK, 1923. Feltman's Restaurant is visible on the right in this view looking east from Wards Bath at West Eleventh Street.

PAUL BAUER. The entrepreneur behind the West Brighton Hotel, Bauer had a vision to create a resort destination at Brighton Beach.

In 1873, William Vanderveer, who had been a bricklayer and plasterer, paid $2,196 for land on the oceanfront, a handsome amount by the standards of the time. On this piece of property, he constructed a three-story hotel and a three-story bathing pavilion plus many bathing houses. Lucy Vanderveer, who had worked at a fruit and confectionery stand on the piazza of the Neptune House, which was located where the Children's Aid Society was to be built, later took over her husband's bathing pavilion. This was a rare opportunity for them. The beaches at this time were prime real estate. The summer season would promise throngs of swimmers and plenty of revenue.

Upon arriving at Coney Island, Garry Katen met with John McKane, and after many promises were made, he built his Beach House next to Ravenhall's. Katen later became McKane's right arm and was put in charge of the common lands. When things got hot for McKane, eyes were focused on Katen. On one occasion when the committee investigating McKane arrived at Katen's gambling establishment and questioned him as to whether he had any idea as to McKane's whereabouts, Katen nodded and said that he would go into the back room and get him. Of course what he did was to go out the back door and walk to Norton's Point, where he took a boat to Staten Island, and just to make sure, he took another boat to New Jersey. Well, he had reason to fear since at one time he had ducked a subpoena.

Paul Bauer, born in Austria on August 18, 1846, made his debut at Coney Island in 1876. He had arrived in New York in 1868 and held many different kinds of employment. He served in the United States Army, where he became a captain in the Fifth Regiment and also a corporal in the Separate Troop. After service in the army, he went back to New York and began work in the restaurant business. His outstanding ability led him to the management of the Van Dyke House and afterwards the Pacific Hotel.

Early in 1876, Bauer took a pleasure ride with his family to Coney Island. Upon arriving at the island, his carriage was almost overturned in a hollow. His wife, whose father was John J. O'Brien, the Republican leader, remarked, "This is the worst place I ever saw." Paul replied, "It can be made the best." Those prophetic words led him with promptness on the following day to secure from the authorities of Gravesend a lease of 12 acres of land fronting on the beach at what today is Brighton Beach.

On February 22, 1876, work began for the erection of the West Brighton Hotel. The hotel, which measured 242 feet long by 145 feet wide, opened on May 2, 1877. Its dining room was capable of seating well over 6,000 people comfortably. There were rooms for over 250 guests, with private dining rooms and four tower rooms that were used for coaching parties. Bauer also opened the Pavilion, which stood across from the hotel. Fine music was played at the hotel each day and evening. Two orchestras, including the famous Vienna Ladies' Orchestra, played at the hotel.

Coney Island was known for its strangeness. Its flat-joints (a carnival concession where gambling is the lure), its mitt-joints (a palm-reader's tent), and

HENDERSON WALK, 1922. This view from Surf Avenue to the Boardwalk displays Coney Island's variety of shops and entertainment.

THE ELEPHANT HOTEL, C. 1890. This unique hotel was built in 1884 on Surf Avenue and burned in 1896.

other kinds of joints all helped to stir the innocent passerby's curiosity. Such a place was James V. Lafferty's "Elephant." The "Elephant" was a colossal structure made to look like an actual elephant. A real elephant would surely never forget or forgive Lafferty for this ridiculous rendition of what is considered the largest land mammal alive. The "Elephant," however, epitomized all the kookey, crazy, loud, immoral, and Victorian "do nots" of Coney Island. The "animal" measured 122 feet from trunk to tail and 6 feet around each leg. It faced the Atlantic across Surf Avenue next to the Sea Beach Palace, which was built in 1879 and served as a railroad depot. Inside the "creature" was a cigar store that took its prime location in one of the front legs, while a diorama was located in the other leg. There were a number of hotel rooms located in principal parts of the body, which of course doubled for all kinds of things. The hotel finally met its end with a blaze of hot fire in 1896.

As Coney's history unveiled, the music played on. At the Sea Beach Hotel, one could hear Calberg's Orchestra, while at Paul Bauer's Hotel, Conterno's Twenty-Third Regiment Band performed. Feltman's offered the Sixth Regiment Band, and at Buel T. Hitchcock's on the Iron Pier, Graffula's Seventh Regiment Band played. At Cable's, Dawning's Ninth Regiment Band with George Washington Arbuckle on his cornet sounded away the evening hours.

Shortly before the Fourth of July, 1895, Captain Paul Boyton opened the Sea Lion Park, the first outdoor amusement park not only in Coney Island, but in the world. Boyton, who had fought in the Civil War and Mexican Revolution, served in 1873 as captain to the first lifesaving service at Atlantic City, New Jersey. Boyton was born in Dublin, Ireland, on June 29, 1848, of American parents. He was raised in Pittsburgh, Pennsylvania, and he first learned to swim in the Allegheny River. He soon followed his father to the West Indies and began to collect, as his father did, shells. The shells were used to make lovely jewelry boxes, which were sold to the public.

Paul Boyton was of an inventive nature. With the aid of C.S. Merriman, a Pittsburgher who worked with rubber, Boyton perfected a rubber suit that contained five internal compartments, which were able to be inflated by blowing into the tubes. This suit was the forerunner to today's frogman suit and astronaut suit. With this suit on, Boyton was able to stay afloat and paddle or swim across the water. Paddling himself at a hundred strokes a minute, he was able to float down the major rivers of the United States and Europe. In addition, he crossed the Strait of Messina in Italy, the Strait of Gibraltar, and finally, after one unsuccessful attempt, he crossed the English Channel.

The wanderlust in him was always evident. His courage, strength, and desire for adventure won him praise from many heads of state. King Alfonso of Spain knighted him and Queen Victoria of England presented him with a gold watch and chain. Medals, scrolls, and jewelry of silver and gold were rewards for his daring feats. As time went on, Boyton improved his rubber suit. He added a sail to the suit to increase speed and a shade cover to protect his eyes from the sun. This "one-man boat" was also aided by a 30-inch boat named *Baby Mine*. This little toy boat carried supplies of water and food.

His suit became so famous that he was invited around the world to exhibit it. Buffalo Bill and his Western Show joined Boyton as part of the show in England. Once, on a return trip to the United States, Boyton was greeted with an 11-gun salute, topped by a personal telegram from President Grant. When he returned in 1894, he leased property at Coney Island and started the Sea Lion Park. He brought back with him from the Caribbean some sea lions, which were put in the pool area of the "Shoot-the-Chutes" ride.

Besides the sea lions, his Sea Lion Park featured a number of interesting new rides. There was the Giant See-Saw, the water races, and the romantic Old Mill. He introduced in America for the first time the famous Shoot-the-Chutes. This ride was a sliding boat or water toboggan that would slide down and land in a pool of water. This type of ride was originally patented in France in 1817 and installed in the Jardin Ruggieri, the famous Parisian amusement park.

Boyton also introduced at his park the Flip-Flap ride, which was a centrifugal cycle railway. It was first exhibited at the Frascati Gardens in Paris, France, in 1848. The French called the ride Chemin du Centrifuge, and Lina Beecher of Batonia, New York, brought the idea to New York in 1898. The first successful centrifugal coaster was erected on Surf Avenue at the corner of West Tenth Street

LUNA PARK, 1922. This view looking toward Luna Park on Surf Avenue from West Tenth Street was taken on December 19, 1922.

in 1901 by Edward Prescott, who came from Arlington, Massachusetts. This same ride was named by Prescott in 1901 the "Loop-the-Loop." In 1902, Captain Boyton closed Sea Lion Park. Money ran out and the season, which lasted 122 days, had had at least 90 days with rain. Boyton sold his park to Thompson and Dundy, who were later to build Luna Park.

Boyton further enjoyed life by building houseboats. He would sail up and down the Mississippi from St. Louis to New Orleans. This part of his life seems rather dull when compared to the time he was offered $5,000 to rescue Captain Alfred Dreyfus in 1896 from Devil's Island. Dreyfus was a Jewish officer in the French army and was framed and convicted as a traitor in 1894. New York Jewish bankers wished to save him, and Boyton was the man they wanted to help in the adventure. Boyton refused to proceed with his plans when Dreyfus's wife begged him not to save him since the authorities of the prison stated that he would be killed if anyone attempted to free him. Upon further investigation by French officials, Dreyfus was later cleared of all charges and released from the prison.

In 1912, Boyton retired and returned to New York to live in the Sheepshead Bay section of Gravesend. "There is one thing about my father when I often think about family life," stated his son Paul Boyton Jr., "if you ever came home from school and said I met Joe Brown or Mary Smith the first words out of his mouth was 'Bring 'em here.' " Boyton Jr., who lived in Sheepshead Bay, added to his description of his father by saying, "For all his knocking around in the world and being a soldier of fortune, I never heard him use a bit of profanity."

On April 18, 1924, Captain Boyton died at his home at 1647 East Twenty-Fourth Street (then Mansfield Place). He had been suffering from pneumonia for three days when he passed away. The funeral services were led by his son Neil, a Jesuit priest, at Saint Mark's Church in Sheepshead Bay, and he was buried at Holy Cross Cemetery on Long Island.

On February 3, 1862, a boy was born in New York City who would later become known as "Mr. Coney Island." His name was George C. Tilyou. He was brought to Coney Island at the age of three by his parents. Tilyou learned about Coney Island life while working at the Surf Bathing Pavilion, where his father, Peter, built a restaurant business by offering a free bowl of clam chowder to every purchaser of a 25¢ bathing ticket.

At the age of 14, George Tilyou was already an expert at crowd psychology. Since people began to come to the island after their visit to the Centennial Exposition of 1876 at Philadelphia, George felt that they should not leave without some kind of memento of Coney. He started selling souvenirs of sifted sand in boxes. By 17, he owned property fronting on the beach. He was a smart real estate salesman, for at once, he began to publish a four-page newspaper called *Tilyou's Telephone*. Tilyou began the paper with one of his original poems, which he called "Sea Sonable"; it reads as follows:

> "Ocean me not," the lover cried,
> "I am your surf—to you I'm tied;
> Don't breaker heart, fair one, but wave
> Objections shine, this sand I crave."
> "Oh billow Bill," she blushed, "I sea
> You would beach ozen shore by me,
> But I'm mermaid not yet in seine,
> And shell for years that way remain."

He concluded the paper with a statement that "If Paris is France, then Coney Island, between June and September, is the World." His paper was able to give a pretty good idea of life at beautiful Coney Island. Anything and everything was for sale at Coney Island, "from a railroad to a lemonade stand," for as little as $25 for a small empty lot to $4,000 for the rent of a hotel. His paper contained the following interesting notes:

> Feltman is getting his large Hotel and Dancing Pavilion in readiness for business, as he anticipates an early season. It is said that the Brighton will introduce American fireworks the coming Summer on their grounds. Stratton and Henderson will open their Sea Side Hotel with a company of first class artists about May 1. De Verna, it is rumored, intends building a large theatre at the island, somewhat after the plans of the Metropolitan Opera House, New York.

A host of advertisements promising to "cure whooping cough and all bronchial and lung diseases" was spread across his paper. There was only one inconspicuous

ENTRANCE TO STEEPLECHASE PARK, C. 1905. This famous park opened in 1897 on 14 acres of land and closed in 1965.

amusement ad, and it read as follows: "Visitors to Coney Island should not fail to ride on the great Flying Boat Coaster in Front of Feltman's Ocean Pavilion."

Young Tilyou was a person of strong character and stamina. On one occasion, he and his father aroused the animosity of John McKane, the town supervisor, who considered them to be disloyal with respect to his political blackmail in dealings with rival real estate dealers. Tilyou nevertheless got along all right and was able to build Coney Island's famous midway, the Bowery.

Inman's Casino and Solomon Perry's Glass Pavilion were just two of the most famous cabarets to dot the Bowery. Others included Connor's Imperial Music Hall, the Trocadero, and the West End Casino. The first showhouse of importance on the island was built by George Tilyou, who named it the Surf Theatre.

Tilyou's greatest claim to fame was the opening of the Steeplechase Park in the spring of 1897. Prior to the launching of the park, he had served the Town of Gravesend as a justice of the peace. Tilyou acquired a new device from a British inventor by the name of J.W. Cawdry. The invention consisted of a mechanical racecourse with metal track, over which large wooden horses ran on wheels, coasting by gravity and climbing by momentum, imitating a horse race. Young lovers were able to snuggle up close to one another as both rode the artificial horse up and down the bumps of the racetrack.

While visiting the Chicago's World's Fair and Columbian Exposition of 1893, Tilyou became very interested in the marvelous invention of G.W.G. Ferris. The invention was the Ferris wheel, 250 feet in diameter with 36 cars able to hold 60 passengers each. He couldn't obtain it for Coney Island since it was going to the St. Louis Fair of 1904. However, he ordered a much smaller wheel that measured 125 feet in diameter with 12 cars, each able to accommodate 18 passengers. The wheel arrived in the spring of 1894. This original Ferris wheel is no longer at Coney Island. The Wonder Wheel, which is at Coney Island today, was built in 1920 at a height of 150 feet, weighing 200 tons, and accommodating 160 passengers.

George Tilyou offered many interesting rides, such as the Aerial Racing Slide, the Intramural Bicycle Railway, and the Double-Dip Chutes. He invented the Human Roulette, which was a round table attached to a motor that turned and turned with great velocity, leaving its passengers in an unstable state. Another of Tilyou's inventions were compressed air jets that blew off men's hats and raised women's dresses and skirts up several inches above the knee.

Tilyou took as a symbol for his Steeplechase a colorful "Funny Face," which exhibited proudly its 44 teeth. After a fire destroyed the Steeplechase in 1907, Tilyou, being consoled by his wife, Mary O'Donnell, rebuilt Steeplechase on a grander scale, expanding it to a much larger amusement area. After the great fire, Tilyou set up the following sign addressed to "Inquiring Friends" outside the ruins: "There was lots of trouble yesterday that I have not had today and there is lots of trouble today that I did not have yesterday." Tilyou charged 10¢ to anyone

Jones Walk, 1922. Seen in the distance is the acclaimed Wonder Wheel. This New York City Landmark is 150 feet tall and holds 160 passengers in 24 cars.

STEEPLECHASE PARK, 1923. After the devastating fire of 1907, Tilyou constructed a steel-and-glass structure to house his various amusement rides.

who wanted to see the remains of the park. Of course, many came since Coney always drew the curious.

Frederic W. Thompson, who was later to be Tilyou's rival at Luna Park, formed a partnership with Elmer (Skip) Dundy and brought to Steeplechase a new invention called a cyclorama, which they named "A Trip to the Moon." This spectacular illusion created the impression of taking off from Earth and traveling to its satellite, the Moon.

Tilyou in time erected a mammoth steel-and-glass structure that placed all his amusements under one large roof. This was a smart move on his part, for on rainy days, the people all came to Steeplechase and thus took business away from Luna Park and Dreamland, Tilyou's rivals.

The Steeplechase added an assortment of amusement rides such as the Wedding Ring, which later became known as the Razzle Dazzel and still later the Hoop-La; the Barrel of Love; the Racing Derby; the Dew Drop, which was a tunnel of love; and the Earthquake Stairway, which was described at the time as "the most unique and side-splitting fun maker in existence." Its flight of steps would split dead center allowing half of the passengers to be jerked up while the other half would descend, permitting the other passengers to go down.

On November 30, 1914, George C. Tilyou passed away, and the entire island mourned his death. Tilyou had served as president of the park, while his younger brother, Edward J. Tilyou, served as secretary. Theodore W. Kramer, who was a good friend of Tilyou, was the vice-president, and James J. McCullough, who was George's brother-in-law, was the treasurer.

High in the belfry of Our Lady of Solace Church, located on Mermaid Avenue and West Seventeenth Street, stands a bell that originally rang from the chimes tower at Steeplechase prior to the 1907 fire. On the bell there is an inscription, which reads as follows:

> We live for those who love us,
> For those whose hearts are true,
> For the God that reigns above us,
> And the good that we may do.

Today, this very bell tower stands as a sounding tribute to a man who made Coney Island his life's work. His park continued after his death, but never with the same spirit as was demonstrated while he was the impresario.

As early as 1884, La Marcus A. Thompson, a roller-coaster inventor (considered in the outdoor amusement world as "the Father of Gravity"), set up a gravity railway called the Switchback, which was the first roller coaster on the island. In the same year, Charles Alcohe set up an oval gravity ride, which was described in *Frank Leslie's Weekly* in 1886 as "a contrivance designed to give passengers, for the insignificant expenditure of five cents, all the sensation of being carried away by a cyclone." In the summer of 1887, a third roller coaster, designed by Philip Hinckle, arrived. La Marcus Thompson was very upset since he was now losing business. He departed Coney Island, fleeing to Atlantic City, New Jersey, where George Tilyou had already opened the Steeplechase Pier. At Tilyou's request, Thompson returned to Coney Island and set up the Scenic Railroad at Steeplechase Park. As time went on, Thompson left Steeplechase and moved across from Surf Avenue, setting up his Pike's Peak Railway.

Hotels, restaurants, saloons, and cabarets opened throughout Coney Island and the neighboring communities of Gravesend with names like Green, Snedeker, Ocean, Van Sicklen, Ravenhall, Shelburne, and Albemarle, which was run by Ben Cohen and stood across Surf Avenue. Whitings' Cabaret, which later became the College Inn, stood on Surf Avenue, while Reisenweher's Restaurant was located off Ocean Parkway. Tom Cable's establishment was known for having the finest wine cellar on the island. The Newark House was run by Louis Stauch, who came to Coney Island in 1877 at the age of 16. Stauch worked for Paul Bauer at first, then worked at Daniel Welch's Saloon, and finally saved enough money to purchase Welch's establishment.

Among the famous entertainers who performed at Stauch's was Israel Baline, who later became the famous Irving Berlin. Jimmy Durante was only 14 years of age when he played the piano at the College Inn at Surf Avenue and West Fifteenth Street for less than $25 a week. Durante also performed at Carey Walsh's Cabaret, singing "I Am Jimmy That Well-Dressed Man." Eddie Cantor and Joe

Matitz started as singing waiters at Walsh's Cabaret. Vincent Lopez's five-man band played at Perry's Cabaret at West Fifteenth Street and the Bowery. The team of Van and Schenck got their professional start at the College Inn. Cary Grant, the famed actor, first started as a vaudeville performer on the island. Erick Weiss, alias Harry Houdini, the famous escape artist who vowed he would return from the dead, worked at Coney Island for $12 a week. Bud Abbott, of the comedy team of Abbott and Costello, lived and worked at Coney Island. He once sold peanuts and popcorn for Marie Dressler, the actress, who was in charge as a publicity drawing card for the peanut and popcorn stands at Dreamland.

George Bader's lovely Roadhouse, which stood at Ocean Parkway and King's Highway, entertained many guests. Gargiulo's Restaurant, which was established in 1907, still serves the community at West Fifteenth Street. The Seventy-First Regiment band played at the famous Riccadona Hotel, which stood on Ocean Parkway opposite the Brighton Beach Music Hall. Duffy's St. Nicholas Hotel, Pabst's Loop Hotel (operated by Frank Clayton), and Dick Gorm's Hotel in the Sea Beach Terminal were other hotels on the island. Martin Dawling's Roadhouse and Mrs. O'Brien's Roadhouse on the Boulevard added to the festive atmosphere. Small little walks were formed around the Bowery, which today stretches from West Sixteenth Street to Jones Walk. Sheridans Walk, Scovilles Walk (now Jones Walk), Kensington Walk, Henderson Walk, and Scheickerts Walk all can still be seen today

CONEY'S ISLAND BOWERY, C. 1895. This celebrated section of Coney Island featured the first Joe's Restaurant. (Courtesy the James A. Kelly Local Historical Studies Institute.)

EMMONS AVENUE, 1934. This image shows the picturesque setting of Sheepshead Bay, with its many restaurants and docks.

Kate Leary, the wife of the famed bank robber John (Red) Leary, operated an inn halfway between The Hermitage, which was run by Joe Gorman, who was a well-known pickpocket and his wife, Molly (the notorious shoplifter), and Moran's Hotel. The first of the famous Joe's Restaurants was located on the Bowery of Coney Island, as was the Greater New York Hotel. Fred Henderson introduced vaudeville at his restaurant and music hall located on Surf Avenue. Other establishments featuring vaudeville acts included the Imperial and Herman Wacke's Trocadero Hotel, which exhibited in 1893 the film *The Wrong Number*, the first moving picture exhibited in the United States. Gilbert and Sullivan operettas were started on the island by Paul Bauer.

The Sheepshead Bay section of Gravesend, which has the appearance of a New England fishing village, had several excellent seafood restaurants. There was the Sheepshead Bay Inn, which was located at Sheepshead Bay Road and Emmons Avenue not too far from the McKeever Mansion, which stood at Emmons and Voorhies. Tappen's Restaurant, which was first established in 1842 as a carriage house to serve clam chowder, was the finest seafood restaurant in all of New York. George Tappen ran it, and on one occasion the famous Charles Dickens ate at the restaurant. Tappen's Hotel was located on Emmons Avenue between East

EMMONS AVENUE, 1937. This bird's-eye view of Sheepshead Bay shows Jamaica Bay in the background and the newly opened Marine Parkway Bridge in the distance.

Twenty-Sixth Street and East Twenty-Seventh Street. Lillian Russell and Diamond Jim Brady were two of the most famous wealthy frequenters at the restaurant.

Big Jim Villepigue, who weighed in at 335 pounds, ran an inn and cottage located on the corner of Voorhies and Ocean Avenue. Villepigue, who first introduced the "Shore Dinner" costing about a $1.25, took over Tappen's. Tappen's Restaurant met its end on May 5, 1950, when fire destroyed the building. It had served the community for almost 106 years. "It was one of the few remaining at the Bay recalling the good old days of the race tracks in the area with remarkable finishes of the immortal Snapper Garrison, and the band concerts of Patrick Sarsfield Gilmore," wrote the *Brooklyn Eagle*. The *Eagle*'s story continued by recording the following:

> Other notables who frequented Tappen's were Alfred Gwynne Vanderbilt, the Goulds, Clarence Mackey, Harry K. Thaw and Fanny Ward. And it was whispered that Caesar Young once reached under a Tappen table to snap the baby-blue garter of his inamorata, Nan Patterson. Ah, those wicked, wicked days!

Truely, the death of Tappen's is the death of a Brooklyn era. Up to the end, the picturesque old restaurant and hotel remained practically the same as when the coaches, barouches, smart traps and tallyhos stopped there with their prominent owners after a day spent at the nearby race track.

A person who had not been to the restaurant between the days of horse cars, spring wagons and oil lamps and this year [1950] would easily recognize Tappen's at once. It had been enlarged somewhat and repairs had been made to the roof. Also modern plumbing and furniture had been installed, but the architecture remained practically the same as the day it was opened by Jeremiah Tappen, a Grand Street, Manhattan hotel keeper, a long time before the Civil War. Then New Yorkers went to Sheepshead Bay by ferry and horse-drawn wagons.

Tappen's was sold in 1948 to Frederick Lundy, owner of Lundy's Restaurant, another famous Sheepshead Bay restaurant. Fred Lundy started his business by just selling clams and oysters wholesale to the Manhattan Beach, Brighton Beach, and Oriental Hotels. His first location was actually a clam bar that was situated on Dooley Street. Lundy, who was at one time registrar of King's County, planted his oysters on Plumb Beach. The establishment later moved to the foot of Ocean Avenue bridge. On one occasion, one of the Lundy's children was kidnapped and held for ransom. His son was finally released after the ransom was paid.

EMMONS AVENUE, 1934. The Lundy Brothers Restaurant is seen here under construction in Sheepshead Bay.

LUNDY BROTHERS RESTAURANT, 1934. The second location of the restaurant was situated on the bay side of Emmons Avenue at the intersection of Ocean Avenue.

After World War I, Irving Lundy and his brother Stanley set up a clam stand, which grew considerably. They kept on adding additions until finally it was taken over by the City when landfilling started. The brothers then moved to the north side of Emmons Avenue and built the present structure, which was completed in 1934.

Other hotels and restaurants at Sheepshead Bay are listed as follows: the Captain's Inn, which stood at 3041 Ocean Avenue; the Jerome Hotel and Restaurant; the Lewis House, at Emmons and Bedford Avenues; the Hotel Beau Rwage; the Nelly Bly Hotel; the Sheirr's Restaurant; Seidel's; and Schuessler's, at Sheepshead Bay Road and East Fifteenth Street. The U.S. Hotel stood south of Voorhies Avenue on Sheepshead Bay Road not far from where the Belmont Inn stood on East Sixteenth Street. Dominick's Hotel was located on a small peninsula that jutted out off Sheepshead Bay Road. Clark's Manhattan House stood at Jerome Avenue and Sheepshead Bay Road where the King's Highway Savings Bank was located. The famous Bay View Hotel served many at its establishment on Emmons Avenue and Sheepshead Bay Road where the Bay View Apartments are situated today. Garden parties were common at Gasgrove's Hotel on Jerome Avenue.

During this period of time, it only cost a nickel to take a rowboat from Sheepshead Bay to Plumb Beach. On the west side of the Brighton Railroad Line stood Irish Town. This community was formed around the 1840s when political unrest and great famines plagued Ireland. Immigration into the United States led the people into King's County as well as the other surrounding counties. Once again, as in the case of Dame Deborah Moody, Gravesend provided a shelter for those who suffered from persecution. Around the same time, a group of the Sons of Erin, many from County Clare, set up a community in the northern part of the Town of Gravesend. They named this section South Greenfield since it was south of the village of Greenfield.

Shortly after the arrival of Brooklyn's first Roman Catholic bishop, John Loughlin, in 1853, the first Catholic parish was established in the Town of Gravesend in 1861. The church was built in the village of Sheepshead Bay on the southeast corner of Sheepshead Bay Road and East Fourteenth Street. The small wooden structure was blessed and named in honor of Saint Mark. This structure was later destroyed by fire and a new edifice of worship was built on Ocean Avenue and Avenue Z.

As years went on, additional parishes were formed in Gravesend. Guardian Angel parish on Ocean Parkway was formed on May 30, 1885; St. Mary Mother of Jesus on June 9, 1889; S.S. Simon and Jude on December 25, 1897; Our Lady of Solace in October 1900; St. Brendan on September 29, 1907; St. Athansius on December 7, 1913; St. Margaret Mary on Ocean Avenue on June 1, 1920; St. Edmund on April 15, 1922; Resurrection in June 1924; Precious Blood in 1927; Good Shepherd on July 1, 1927; and Our Lady of Grace on Avenue W on January 6, 1935.

In 1877, Alanson Treadwell arrived at Sheepshead Bay from Manhattan, where he had been a successful merchant. He purchased some property located on

ST. MARK'S CHURCH, C. 1900. This historic church was located on the southeast corner of East Fourteenth Street. (Courtesy the James A. Kelly Local Historical Studies Institute.)

Emmons Avenue east of East Twenty-Seventh Street near the waterfront. There was some difficulty with the property since it was marshy. Treadwell filled it in and built huge, beautiful summer homes upon the new land. With time, this area grew and many more homes were added until it became known as Lincoln Beach. Since the inhabitants were all wealthy, it later became known as "Millionaires Row." Some of these homes are still in existence today, although they have undergone numerous changes and repairs. The Barge Restaurant (at 2912 Emmons Avenue) and the Sheepshead Bay Yacht Club (the summer home of Albert and Julius Liebmann, who were owners of the Rheingold Brewery) are just two of the many buildings left from the days of the "Great Gatsby."

Sheepshead Bay was originally known as "The Cove" and retained its tranquil rural atmosphere until Ocean Parkway and Coney Island Avenue were built. How many can remember the old Celtic Park, which was located at Sheepshead Bay Road and East Thirteenth Street where the Atlantic Towers Apartments now stand? Or perhaps, McLoughlin's Casino, which had a lovely balcony overlooking the Bay and a ballroom that was filled with the music of Vincent Lopez's band?

Today, the newly renovated Lundy's Restaurant, which was declared a landmark in March 1992 and reopened in October 1994, stands on the site of the former casino. The famous Billie Burke, who later married Lawrence Ziegfield, the theatrical entrepreneur, was born and bred in Sheepshead Bay. The two McGeeber brothers, who lived on Sheepshead Bay Road near where the Belt Parkway is located, were greatly responsible for the creation of the now-extinct Brooklyn Dodgers.

LUNDY BROTHERS RESTAURANT, 1934. This is a view of the present-day structure of the Lundy Brothers Restaurant during the time of its construction.

COX'S HOTEL AND BATHS AND OCEAN BATHS, 1922. *These popular bathing establishments were located near West Tenth Street.*

Some of the street names in Sheepshead Bay were changed to numbered streets as the street system changed in Brooklyn. Mansfield Place became East Twenty-Fourth Street while Delamere Place became East Twenty-Third Street; Elmore Place, East Twenty-Second Street; and Kenmore Place, East Twenty-First Street.

Coney Island grew further and so did its craziness. There was Professor King's Captive Balloon, a hot air ballon which "defied gravity." Up the people went, not knowing whether to believe the wise saying: "What goes up must come down." The Inexhaustible Cow served both milk for the kiddies and beer for the adults. Men would gather around in a semi-circle to watch the bumps and sensual movements of Little Egypt, the belly dancer who arrived from the Columbian Exposition of Chicago in 1895. An original replica of the streets of Cairo was set up on the corner of Surf Avenue and West Tenth Street in 1897.

As time went on, Norton's Point became the home of Gugliermo Marconi's Wireless Station, which was operated by David Sarnoff, who later became both the president and chairman of the Radio Corporation of America (RCA).

The great bathing houses at the island drew many people and included Balmer's Atlantic Bathing and Swimming, Stauch's Baths, Oriole Baths, Irving Baths, Ocean Baths, Washington Baths, and Cox's Baths. Taking baths was a luxurious experience many years ago. It is often taken for granted that today everyone has a bathtub and hot running water at home. In the past, one did not have these facilities at home and so the people came to the bathing houses to cleanse and refresh themselves—very much like the Romans at the Baths of Caracalla.

The Atlantic Yacht Club, which was located at Beach Fiftieth at Sea Gate, was organized in 1866 and was considered Brooklyn's leading yacht club. Commodore Harrison B. Moore headed the club, which had a membership of over 700. The Brooklyn Canoe Club was located at Bay Forty-Eighth Street and Gravesend Bay. The Brooklyn Yacht Club stood at the foot of Bay Thirty-Third Street, which is now Twenty-Third Avenue. There was also the Gravesend Bay Yacht Club, which was located at the base of Ulmer Park. Today, Gravesend can still boast about its yacht clubs. Some of them are as follows: the Sheepshead Bay Yacht Club, on Emmons Avenue; the Excelsior Yacht Club, at the foot of Twenty-Sixth Avenue; the Little Venice Yacht Club, at the Shell Bank Creek; the Miramar Yacht Club, on Emmons Avenue; the Varuna Boat Club, also on Emmons Avenue; and the Ben McChree Boat Club, on Shore Parkway.

The first World Championship Prizefight to be held in the State of New York was held at Coney Island on June 9, 1899. The Coney Island Athletic Club sponsored the fight, as it did many other fights at Coney Island. Jim Corbett and Charley Mitchell, who came from England, fought for the heavyweight championship. On November 3, 1899, Tom Sharkey, the one-time sailor who lived on Voorhies Avenue, and Jim Jeffries, the one-time boiler-maker, fought it out for 25 rounds, which was considered by many at the time as the longest and most malicious, bloodthirsty fight in history. It was a common sight to see on the beach Bob Fitzsimmons, the prizefighter, walking majestically with his lion. Prizefighting was getting out of hand not only because it was considered cruel, but illegal gambling was taking place and there were those who stood to gain from the fighting matches. People began complaining to the politicians to the point that Governor Theodore Roosevelt signed the Horton Act, which brought prizefighting to a grinding halt in New York State.

EMMONS AVENUE, 1938. Many local boaters enjoyed the waters provided by Sheepshead Bay, Gravesend, and Coney Island.

JOHN Y. MCKANE. McKane was a significant figure in Gravesend's history, serving as town supervisor from 1879 to 1894.

While Coney Island grew with all its laughter and tears, there was one individual, however, who was the omnipotent ruler who controlled all that happened on the island. Coney Island and the rest of Gravesend were like a marionette under this local deity's handiwork. He made the community go up and he made it go down like the surrounding waves. He made it laugh and he made it cry. This demagogue was none other then John Y. McKane, the political tyrant of Gravesend, ruling from 1879 to 1894. Why, just the mere mention of his name brought chills to many people who lived and walked in his path.

From Eire, Ireland, he came as a child to the United States leaving his native County Antrim. He grew up in the Town of Gravesend and worked as a clam-digger at Sheepshead Bay. He was a carpenter and a builder, as was his father before him. As a private citizen and as a businessman, McKane was an admirable person.

On the first Tuesday in April 1867 at the annual civic meeting, John McKane was elected with the smallest vote as the third constable of Gravesend. He was also chosen as the superintendent of the Methodist Episcopal Church and was later to be made a deacon. McKane was assiduous in attendance at services and lavishly generous in support of the minister and church charities. As constable, he collected the rents of the common lands, and he later became the commissioner of the common lands. McKane was "a one-man everything," from Sunday school teacher to chief of police. He was an ex-officio chairman of the Town Board, Board of Health, the Water Board, the Improvement Board, and the Board of Audit.

McKane's power in Gravesend was comparable, if not greater, than Brooklyn's Boss Hugh McLoughlin and Tammany's William Marcy Tweed (Boss Tweed), both his friends. William J. Gaynor, who later became mayor of Greater New York, was the lawyer for the Trustees of Gravesend's common lands. At one point, his career almost came to an end thanks to McKane. Reports of frauds in Gravesend over the land commissioners' dealings with the common lands brought Gaynor into the limelight since he was in charge of the title closings. He knew all that was going on behind the scenes, but never bothered to criticize McKane, for he felt that some day he would need all the support he could get from McKane and his cronies.

Gaynor had to testify that he had no crooked dealings, although a witness had testified that he gave a $3,500 check to him. The witness claimed that in return he received a deed for a plot of land on Coney Island's oceanfront. On the deed, the price of sale was marked $2,500 and those investigating the matter wanted to know where the missing $1,000 went. So Gaynor had explained, "I have nothing to conceal. I have been here twelve years at this bar and it is painful to me even to come here and explain this matter, because I have never been asked to explain anything I did before. I will tell you all that I had to do with it so as to get to the end of it."

As it turned out, he was truly innocent of the matter and he was spared prosecution. But it looked very bad for McKane. The Democratic Party of King's County punished McKane by temporarily throwing him out of the party, but soon enough McKane got even. As town supervisor, McKane was able to control the voting of the people. There were six voting districts in Gravesend, and McKane was smart enough to make sure that the voting districts converged at the Town Hall, which was built in 1873 and was located on the southeast corner of Gravesend Neck Road and McDonald Avenue.

The Town Hall was a two-story structure topped by an ornate bell tower. It had a large public hall with stage and anterooms on the top floor. The first floor contained a courtroom and a room for public business. Several smaller side-rooms were used by the town clerk and other town officers. In the basement stood four cells for the confinement of criminals. On the Gravesend Neck Road side of the building, McKane placed six doors, each representing one of the six election districts of his bailiwick. All six polling places led to the central part of the edifice, which was the hub of the wheel from which their lateral boundaries started. At voting time, there were six ballot boxes constantly under his eye. After a voter left the box, he would often open the box to see whether or not a voter had cast his ballot according to orders.

On Election Day, in 1888, McKane got even with the Democratic Party. He ordered that everyone was to vote Republican, and so as the carriages pulled up at the Town Hall, each person voted one by one as McKane greeted them. Kenneth F. Sutherland, the "Little Corporal" who was his right-hand man, and Dick Newton, who served, as did Sutherland, as justice of the peace, guarded and supervised the voting as McKane proceeded to cross Gravesend Avenue

GRAVESEND TOWN HALL, C. 1873. *Located on the southeast corner of Gravesend Neck Road and McDonald Avenue, this historic structure was built in 1873, served later as a home for the local fire department, and was demolished in January 1913.*

JOHN Y. McKANE ASSOCIATION, 1889. The members are posing in front of Brooklyn's City Hall (present-day Borough Hall) for this picture before their departure for Washington, D.C. in celebration of President Benjamin Harrison's inauguration.

(McDonald Avenue) west a few yards to the Gravesend Cemetery. With paper and pen in hand, McKane began copying here and there a name or two from some of the tombstones, adding them when he got back to Town Hall to the list of those who voted in the election. As it turned out, Gravesend's entire vote went to Benjamin Harrison, thus helping in the defeat of the incumbent Grover Cleveland, who McKane had helped get elected in 1884 by the same method. Thus, Jacobus Lake, though he was dead since 1865, had voted both in 1884 for a Democrat and in 1888 for a Republican. Cleveland may have won the election had it not been for the little town of Gravesend, which cost him 1,000 votes!

As soon as Harrison's winning was confirmed, McKane marched his John Y. McKane Association to the steps of Brooklyn's City Hall, which today is Borough Hall. Each member was dressed in a gray Prince Albert coat with "high-yeller" gloves and a stovepipe hat. As they held their canes in hand, the camera snapped their picture. Soon they were off to Washington, where they took part in Harrison's inauguration. There, they marched down Pennsylvania Avenue in the parade. When they reached the reviewing stand, the President acknowledgingly saluted them by tipping his hat and bowing. Twirling his cane, McKane removed his hat and in a godfatherly manner smiled back at the President.

As chief of police, McKane made up the law to fit his needs. With his diamond-studded badge, he paraded up and down the beaches to make sure that no "funny business" was going on. This short and rather stocky character made sure that the bathing suits on the beach were uniform and that no private parts of the anatomy were showing. Maroon and blue were the official colors of the bathing suits at the beach according to Doctor Durant, who insisted that "the bathing dress should be made of a woolen fabric."

This Victorian attitude was further enforced when orders went out from McKane to arrest any man who didn't wear a shirt. By the end of the first day, the jail was packed. The men, however, were released after spending the night in jail. God forbid if one were caught getting undressed on the beach! All kinds of problems resulted from that act. McKane insisted that no one was to "give Coney a bad name," and just to make sure it had a good name, he set up his own police force.

McKane did much and saw much. On one occasion, he attended a funeral for one of his old friends who was a gambler afflicted with palsy. The old man's final wish was that at his funeral all his friends were to be present in "good spirit." And so as the hearse drove up to the Gravesend Cemetery, the laughing and swaying procession of friends followed. Each tried to keep a straight face but when Joe Gorman, an old friend of the deceased knelt to say a prayer and fell into the grave on top of the coffin, well, that was it, for the laughter could not be contained.

Boss McKane permitted gambling and prostitution on the island. Of course this did not sit too well with Anthony Comstock of the Society for the Suppression of Vice. "The Gut" was a section in Coney Island of wooden shanties that stood between West First and West Third Streets. Here lived the jockeys and exercise boys of the nearby race racks. It was a place of merriment and carnal action and would resemble any corner of New York City's Forty-Second Street before the clean-up. Throughout his shenanigans, McKane was kept very busy.

GRAVESEND OFFICER GERARD W. RYDER, C. 1890s. Wearing several different hats in the community, McKane served as chief of police during his tenure of Gravesend influence.

85

THE BRIGHTON BEACH RACE COURSE, C. 1900. The race course opened in 1879 between Brighton First Street and Coney Island Avenue and closed in 1909. (Courtesy the New York Racing Association.)

In the latter part of the nineteenth century, not only were there three main hotels developing but also three money-making race tracks. Horse racing began in Gravesend in 1868, when the Prospect Park Ground and Race Course was set up in the northeastern part of the town. It was a 1-mile track containing nearly 60 acres. The large clubhouse for the track was built near Gravesend Avenue, now McDonald Avenue. Around 1874, a half-mile track was built near Parkville with some 40 acres of land. In 1883, this track became the New York and Brooklyn Driving Club and stood north of King's Highway.

The sport of horse racing in New York State, however, can be traced back to the year 1665. In that year, Governor Richard Nicolls introduced racing in the colony "for encouraging the bettering of the breed of horses, which, through neglect had been impaired." The first course was set up at Hempstead Plains and was named by Nicolls, "Newmarket." Racing continued uninterrupted until the Revolutionary War.

It was not until 1879 that true horse racing had its start in Gravesend. In that year, William A. Engeman, the builder of Brighton Beach, formed the Brighton Beach Race Course, which was located between Ocean Parkway and Coney Island Avenue on the east and the west and between Sheepshead Bay Road and Sea Breeze Avenue on the north and south. Racing began at the course on June 28, 1879, and resumed in July. Attendance was great, and more meetings were held. All in all, there were six meetings at the track in the first year with over 34 days of racing.

As the years went on, racing continued with greater numbers of people arriving and betting. In 1897, Engeman died, and his son, William Engeman Jr., took over the track and improved the grounds, building an entirely new grandstand. C.J. Fitzgerald managed the track until 1909, when the track closed for races. The track was later to be used for flying airplanes. On August 2, 1908, Henri Farman, a bicycle-automobile racer who made the first circular flight in Europe three years after the Wright Brothers' first circle, took his plane off the ground from the track for a third of a mile in 30 seconds.

On June 19, 1880, Gravesend's second race track opened; it was named the Coney Island Jockey Club (Sheepshead Bay Race Track) and was located between Ocean Avenue and Haring Street and Avenue V and Avenue X approximately. Costing nearly $135,000 to complete, it covered nearly 125 acres of land that was once known as "Neck Woods." The founding fathers of the track included Leonard W. Jerome (father of Jenny Jerome, who was the mother of Sir Winston Churchill), John Heckscher, August Belmont, General Daniel Butterfield, James G. Lawrence, Pierre Lorillard Jr., James V. Parker, A.B. Purdy, A. Wright Sanford, F.A. Schermerhorn, George Peters, Shipworth Gordon, Henry Alexandre, and William K. Vanderbilt.

Of the three racetracks located in Gravesend, the Coney Island Jockey Club was the most exclusive. The lovely paddock of the club with its extensive enclosure was reserved for the horse-owners, club members, and their friends. The track itself seated well over 5,000. The Gold Room at the club was often visited by James R. Keene (considered the leading money-winning horse owner),

CONEY ISLAND JOCKEY CLUB, C. 1898.
This photograph captures the racers in mid-stride, a crowd of anxious spectators, and the judges' stand. (Courtesy the New York Racing Association.)

WHITNEY RESIDENCE, 1920. This beautiful house was the home of William C. Whitney, former secretary of the U.S. Navy.

Robert Pinkerton, William C. Whitney (the English Derby winner and leading horse owner in America as well as the former secretary of the U.S. Navy), and Diamond Jim Brady.

The track offered three races. The 6-furlong Futurity was considered America's richest race ever at $40,900. The inaugural race had a field of 14, and it was won by Proctor Knott, Haggin's Salvator was second, and Galen came in third. The Futurity left Sheepshead Bay and went to Saratoga in 1910, then to Belmont from 1915 to 1958, and finally to Aqueduct. The track also had the Suburban, which was the country's leading handicap, and Realization, which was begun in 1889.

The first meeting at the track lasted for six days, and some of the sweepstakes included the Coney Island Handicap, the Coney Island Derby, the Foam, the Surf, the Tidal, and the Mermaid. Some of the more famous jockeys included Henry Spencer (alias Iceman), riding Cap and Bell; Milton Henry, riding Olympian; Winnie O'Connor, riding Tommy Atkins; Tod Sloan, riding Ballyhoo Bey; Snapper Garrison, riding Tenny; Isaac Murphy, riding Salvator; and Jimmy Fitzsimmons, riding Agnes D. Jimmy Fitzsimmons started his career in horse racing as an exercise boy in 1885. Exercise boys were very important. They cared for the horses by exercising and grooming them. His father's farm adjoined the property of the track and every day after leaving Public School 98, which was near the track, he would stop in at the stables and check on the horses. By 1889, he was a jockey.

The Coney Island Jockey Club, which really stood in Sheepshead Bay, expanded itself and in 1886 added a turf course. William S. Vosburg in his book *Racing in America 1866–1921* describes the club in the following manner: "The club members' badges were of metal and both artistic and unique in design, a sea shell, a jockey cap, or a horse's head in enamel with the club's initials; its entry books in colors representing the finish of great races. The club had a flower girl and the winner of the Coney Island Derby was expected to present her with clothing of his stable."

The final meeting at the track was held in 1910 due to the legislation enacted against horse racing, and the club folded up in 1916. The track, however, was still used before it was demolished. On October 17, 1915, the Astor Cup Race, a car race, was held there, and in 1918 Enrico Caruso, the famous Italian opera tenor, sang at the track for police games that were held at the track. Thousands of people cheered Caruso and his newly wedded wife, Dorothy.

One of the more interesting and historic events to occur at the track came on a Sunday in mid-September 1911, when Calbraith Perry Rodgers left the track in a Wright biplane for what was to be a world's-record flight from coast to coast. The day was sunny and warm, and nearly 2,000 spectators gathered. The plane was christened the *Vin Fiz Flyer* after a grape drink that was poured over the plane. Rodgers finally started up the plane and within minutes after gaining speed, the tiny *Vin Fiz* left the earth and ascended into the white-clouded, azure sky. Eighty-four days later, after one broken ankle and nearly five crashes, Cal Rodgers arrived at Long Beach, California. Cal's plane was rebuilt and repaired so many times that

THE GRANDSTAND OF THE CONEY ISLAND JOCKEY'S CLUB, C. 1900. Located between Ocean Avenue and Haring Street and between Avenues V and X, the club opened in 1880 and closed as a race track in 1910. (Courtesy the New York Racing Association.)

CONEY ISLAND JOCKEY'S CLUB. These workers are seen here during a relaxing moment outside of the stables.

only the engine drip pan and the rudder remained from the original plane that had left the track. His historic plane trip made him the first man to cross the United States and the first ever to have flown that incredible distance.

The third racetrack came into existence in August 1886. Michael G. Dwyer and Philip J. Dwyer, who were once in the butcher business, organized the Brooklyn Jockey Club at the track that became known as the Gravesend Race Track. The track stood between Ocean Parkway and Gravesend Avenue (McDonald Avenue) and between King's Highway and Avenue U. The Dwyer brothers purchased the property that was once used by the Prospect Park Ground and Race Course (Prospect Park Fair Grounds Association), and almost immediately the response was positive. On one occasion, Edna Wallace Hopper, the famous actress, rented the track for one day all for herself.

A law was set up by the State of New York regulating racing in the state. This law became known as the Ives Law of 1887. The law called for the following:

> a tax of five per centum upon the gross amounts of the receipts for admission on race days, to race tracks or grounds on which racing is had, owned, leased or conducted by a racing association incorporated under the laws of the State of New York. . . . that such racing and pool selling in this state shall be confined to the period between the 15th day of May

and the 15th day of October in each year, and all pool selling shall be confined to the track where the races take place, and on the days when the races take place.

Pool selling had its problem, and John McKane was there. McKane knew that horse racing and gambling were synonymous, and so he allowed bookies and pool rooms to operate freely in the Town of Gravesend. Pool-selling was a method of gambling on horses. It was succeeded by bookmaking and today there are off-track betting storefronts where adults can test their fate at betting on horses without being at the track.

However, problems arose with Western Union. The company was paying about $1,700 to the race tracks for furnishing the results of the races to the New York pool rooms. The Gravesend Track felt that they should be getting paid more, but Western Union felt that it was paying enough and therefore refused any increase. At this time, all kinds of tricks began to formulate between the company and

BOOKMAKERS AT THE BROOKLYN JOCKEY CLUB, C. 1906. The club opened in 1886 and closed in 1910. (Courtesy the New York Racing Association.)

CONEY ISLAND JOCKEY'S CLUB, C. 1895. This club had a 1-mile track and later reopened as the Sheepshead Bay Raceway. (Courtesy the New York Racing Association.)

Gravesend. Western Union started sending spies and agents down to the track who would signal the winner to other spies in designated locations, and they in return telephoned the winner in, sometimes even before the race was completely over.

At the Brighton Beach track, the Iron Observatory was an excellent lookout. A person with field glasses could very easily see what was happening and send signals. The Pinkerton detectives became wise to this, and McKane started arresting the signalers. These signalers were kept in jail for several days by order of Judge Sutherland and then they were dismissed.

Finally, an investigation was called, and the *Brooklyn Eagle*, on September 26, 1891, reported the following news item:

> The grand jury will be called upon to investigate the scenes which occurred at the late meeting of the Brooklyn Jockey Club at Gravesend and the connection therewith of Chief of Police John Y. McKane, Justice Kenneth Sutherland and Bob Pinkerton in charge of the track.

The investigation failed to prove any wrong-doing and things continued just the same. At the Brooklyn Jockey Club, Philip Dwyer locked the gates and permitted no one to leave until the last race was over. Fights broke out and another investigation took place and once again nothing happened. People still came to the track by railroad, trolley, four-in-hands, and buggies, all dressed and prepared for the races. By 1894, the Brooklyn Jockey Club paid $21,946 in taxes under the Ives

Law, while the Brighton Beach Track paid $16,546.57 and the Coney Island Jockey Club, $27,607.89.

During this period of time, people dressed formally. There was a certain etiquette that was required and maintained, regardless of what social class one belonged. Horse racing was regarded as a leisure activity; however, the people still upheld a formal air and pride for this form of entertainment. The same was true for going to the beach. Every man wore a suit with a straw hat during the summer.

In 1895, Governor Morton recommended the Grey-Percy Law and stated that "it was probably not intended by the Constitutional Amendment to prohibit racing altogether, but the evil of pool-selling and book-making had become so great that the Constitutional Convention of 1894 felt justified in recommending the adoption of a constitutional provision against it." But still the practice continued, and on May 26, 1906, the *New York Times* reported the following under the headlines: "Poolrooms Get News from Gravesend Tract / Won't Tell How, but Proprietors / Say It's 'All Fixed.' / Nothing Is Lacking on Any Race and the / Managers Say This Will Continue."

> For the first time since the racing season opened in the East, the New York poolrooms obtained an adequate service from the track yesterday. There was not the slightest hitch in securing advance information of Gravesend events, and there were no errors as to scratches, prices, jockeys, and overweights. A description was given of every event as it was run off, and the descriptions tallied accurately with the published charts.
>
> There was not only first betting, but post betting, and the poolroom managers seemed to have not the slightest hesitancy about taking bets right up to post time. How they got their services nobody knew but themselves and they wouldn't tell.
>
> Poolroom patrons were delighted. The wretched service from Gravesend on Thursday had them guessing. There were errors as to every race, and in one or two of the events, no pretense was made to post track odds.
>
> "We'll pay off by ticker odds," the managers announced, "or bettors can be paid off tomorrow on newspaper odds."
>
> When the time came for posting the first yesterday afternoon an entire change had come over the situation. The scratches were posted, the jockeys being shown ten minutes before post time. In some of the rooms, it is true, the jockeys were posted as "probable," but this precaution was unnecessary.
>
> As race followed race and there were no errors in the service, the poolroom men became radiant with joy. After the last race they issued a proclamation to their patrons.
>
> "Our troubles are over now," they said, "and from now on we'll deliver the goods as we used to do in the past."

REMAINS OF THE STABLES OF THE CONEY ISLAND JOCKEY'S CLUB, 1929. Located on the northeast corner of Avenue Y and Batchelder Street, the stables fell into disrepair after the club closed in 1910.

The article continued, quoting the manager of one of the big uptown rooms, saying the following to a player:

"Until this morning, we didn't know that we would be up against the Belmont-Slicer agreement all summer. There is no doubt about the fact that The Jockey Club can so hamper us, if it desires, that there will be nothing like the money in our game which is required to operate at a profit.

"We got the word last night, after about the worst day we have had, that things had been fixed, and that there would be no difficulty today or any other day hereafter. I was a little doubtful, as the tip to this effect had been handed around before and failed to materialize. When the first race came in today, though, I knew that we had gotten the straight information.

"We have had a pretty hard row to hoe since the season opened at Aqueduct. No poolroom player wants to put his money down until he knows the starters and the jockeys. As long as they kept the scratches and jockeys away from us, our play was not within fifty per cent of what it ought to be. Yesterday was the first good day we have had."

It was indeed a good day for the rooms, for there wasn't a player in all New York who had not a tip on Ram's Horn to win the Parkway Handicap. Had the Williams colt come in first, the rooms would have been badly scorched. As it was, they cleaned up handsomely. Indeed, they got few bad breaks on the Gravesend track, the winning of Consistent in the third event leaving them with a clean sheet. A handsome profit was shown on the Yorkshire Lad race. Nearly all the poolroom players went to Glen Echo or Red Friar in that event.

"Come around tomorrow, boys," was the parting remark of the poolroom keepers. "You'll find everything all right, just as it was today. Our troubles are over."

Their "troubles" were not over. William Randolph Hearst, who was running for office as governor of the state, swore that if he was elected he would get rid of betting forever. He lost the election, but the winner, Charles Evans Hughes, to the amazement of all, proposed legislation against horse racing, and it was enacted in 1909.

In 1910, the Brooklyn Jockey Club closed as did the other tracks forever because of the illegal practices that took place—cheating being one of them. Thus, Gravesend as a town began to lose its notoriety. Not only did the racetracks disappear, but also the wealthy and affluent who frequented them. Economically speaking, Gravesend was going into a financial crisis.

With the closing of the racetracks, the three large hotels were beginning to feel the pains of diminishing numbers of customers. The Manhattan Beach Hotel, which stood at the beach between where Beaumont and Exeter Streets are today, was razed in 1911. The Oriental Hotel, standing on the beach between where Irwin and Kensington Streets are located today, was demolished in 1916. The Brighton Beach Hotel, which was moved back 600 feet inland from the encroaching sea in 1888, was finally demolished in 1924.

On April 3, 1888, work began to move the 6,000-ton Brighton Beach Hotel. The hotel measured nearly 500 feet long and had 300 rooms accommodating nearly 600 guests. Six train engines were needed to move the hotel along 24 iron rails. One hundred twenty-five iron flat-cars were placed under the hotel. This miraculous feat, under the engineering supervision of George Farquhar, was

MOVING THE BRIGHTON BEACH HOTEL, 1888. This early photograph shows some of the materials and manpower needed to move the luxury resort.

completed on June 29, 1888, at a cost of nearly $80,000. This hotel was located between Brighton Fifth Street and Coney Island Avenue.

While the hotels and race tracks were still in their prime, John McKane continued his daily work. Grading, construction, and improvements of roads were very important tasks that had to be done. The Board of Supervisors of King's County provided a resolution making such work possible. With the approval of the supervisor-at-large, certain commissioners were appointed by the Supreme Court for the purpose of opening, enlarging, improving, grading, and the constructing of streets. For example, on December 18, 1885, with the approval of McKane, J.D. Costigan, Edmund Williams, and S. Stryker Williamson were sworn in to act as opening commissioners for West Fifth Street.

Orgies, prostitution, and promiscuity were constant on the island and the one man behind it all was McKane. McKane believed that "houses of prostitution are a necessity on Coney Island." Others disagreed, and on a Saturday morning in March 1887 in the chamber of the Brooklyn Common Council, McKane was subpoenaed to report on this issue. Alexander Bacon, a Brooklyn Republican, served as the chairman of the committee investigating the wrongdoings on the island. John Parsons served as the chief counsel. This committee's mission was to uncover McKane's corruption. McKane denounced all and said he knew nothing of the wrongdoings. Around the room stood his cronies and others who dared not to speak out against him since he had control of their mortgages for the property they owned. One after one, the witnesses went up and claimed ignorance to the charges in sincerity or in perjury.

One witness, however, charged McKane with bribery and fraud. This witness stated that he had to pay McKane a $4,000 bribe to purchase a piece of land. McKane never denied this. The hearings continued day after day. Things looked especially bad for McKane when George Tilyou, who had yet to build Steeplechase Park, spoke the greatest accusations. Knowing full well that McKane would get him for it, he told the committee all he knew about the houses of prostitution and how McKane hired doctors for $2 a week to check the prostitutes. A Pandora's box was opened over Gravesend's town supervisor and there was no way to close it. McKane's temper was up, and he demanded to make a statement.

On May 11, 1887, the committee agreed that Coney Island was "a source of corruption and crime" and that it was "disgraceful and dangerous." McKane was considered "an enemy, and not a friend, of the administration of justice." The committee was very upset and they called for "the immediate indictment and the prompt prosecution of John McKane, in order that, if convicted, he may not be punished but removed from the offices whose trust he has so completely betrayed." They further recommended that the Town of Gravesend be made part of the City of Brooklyn. McKane chuckled at their recommendations, for he felt he had nothing to fear since Hugh McLaughlin, the Brooklyn Boss, would protect him. McKane was victorious this time, but it wasn't long before his "Swan Song" would be sung.

After the election of 1888, McKane's election practices were held suspect. William Gaynor, who lost the nomination as mayor of the City of Brooklyn to David A. Boody, began an investigation of McKane's practices stating that "six thousand men do not vote in Gravesend, but the names of waiters, gamblers, and thieves [he left out the deceased citizens] from all over the country are checked off. I say to these people that I defy them."

These accusations proved factual, for Gaynor found the truth out when a bartender from Coney Island explained that McKane would register the people who came to Coney Island in the summer. He forced them to register as permanent residents of the Town of Gravesend and ordered them to vote in Gravesend on Election Day. They complied with his wishes out of fear, for they wanted to return the following summer to the beaches of Coney Island and conduct their businesses.

Gaynor had to move fast since Election Day was only a few days away. At this election, he was to be voted on for justice of the Supreme Court, and he wanted to make sure that McKane would in no way "fix things up" to ensure his defeat. Gaynor wanted to check the registration lists of Gravesend. McKane, of course, prevented this but wrote that he had nothing to do with the registration lists or the prevention of access to them and in fact he claimed he had sent John Wesley Murphy, his secretary, to tell Gaynor that he would give him a copy of the lists.

On November 2, 1888, Gaynor applied for a mandamus writ, which was later denied the next day by Supreme Court Justice A.M. Cullen. Justice Cullen refused to issue it since he had ordered the voting inspectors to procure the lists. Meanwhile, Gaynor wrote letters to some of the people who he knew were illegally registered. His letter read as follows:

> In fairness to you, I beg to inform you that your connection with the registration and voting in Gravesend is known to me, as well as the number of men which you handle. Being advised, you may take whatever course you see fit.

Gaynor once again requested a mandamus writ but McKane's lawyer temporarily postponed it. Finally, a writ was issued by Justice Cullen ordering the Gravesend Board of Voters to give over the list as soon as possible, excepting on Sunday. Gaynor moved fast, and almost at once he sent 21 men to Gravesend.

That night, the small steam train pulled up at Gravesend Neck Road and Gravesend Avenue and the men stepped out. Fireworks exploded, ignited by McKane. Clubs and fists were flying, and when it was over, nearly 14 of Gaynor's men were carried off to the Coney Island police station. Justice Sutherland booked them as troublemakers, and John P. McNamara, the leader of Gaynor's group, was arrested as being intoxicated. The other seven men got away and immediately reported to Gaynor.

All 14 men spent the night in jail, and when daylight came, Sutherland ordered them for a trial in the General Sessions Court on Monday. No bail was set, and they were transported from Gravesend to the downtown Raymond Street jail. Sutherland temporarily left the area, and when Edward Grout, a partner of Gaynor, went to the jailhouse in Coney Island, he found only Richard Newton, who said that "Sutherland was the man to see." Since Sutherland couldn't be found, Grout pleaded with Newton, who politely responded, "I don't give a damn."

McKane had won this time, but still Gaynor would not give up. Election Day was the following day, and the poll watchers were starting to make preparations. Gaynor, when asked what his next step would be, responded as follows:

> I shall have twenty-five detectives in Gravesend tomorrow, and the polls will be watched as they have never been watched before. Every move of McKane and his henchmen will be noted, and if there is any wrongdoing it will be seen. In addition, I have commissioned two watchers to be inside each polling place. McKane may throw them out, but if he does he will provide a means of redress.

Just to make sure that things went well, Gaynor got an injunction issued by Supreme Court Justice Joseph F. Barnard. The injunction would serve to prevent any interference by McKane with his 18 election inspectors. Meanwhile, McKane was making plans for the election also. At his Court Street office in Brooklyn, news reporters questioned him about the previous Saturday night incident. When told that "Gaynor's gang" was released, he responded to them in the following manner:

> Well, we'll arrest them on warrants containing other charges for their actions of Saturday night. Why, a man would have been justified in shooting them on sight on suspicion of their being burglars. When the train arrived, these thugs, sneak-thieves, and crooks walked into the arms of the police [his police], whom I had ordered to be drawn up in front of the town hall to preserve the peace.

McKane was a strong believer in Brooklyn's motto, "Eendraght Maakt Magt," which literally means, "Might Makes Right."

When told that Gaynor was going to send poll watchers on Election Day to Gravesend, he responded by stating the following:

> We'll give them the same kind of reception we gave the ruffians that came down on Saturday night. We'll be able to take care of everyone who has no business in Gravesend. They say a hundred and fifty are coming. Well, they can make it fifteen hundred or fifteen thousand for all I care. We'll take care of them all. We are law-abiding people and we don't propose to have our voters intimidated by anybody.

McKane was stubborn and persistent. One could almost compare him to the former president of the Transit Workers Union, Mike Quill, who for over two weeks in January 1965 held a strike of New York City's public transportation. The city died. People were stranded, and to make matters worse, there was a snowstorm that further complicated matters. When told that he would go to jail if he didn't call his men back to work, Quill responded in a brogue: "May the judge drop dead in his black robes." How ironic that was, for shortly after that statement, Quill was taken to jail and died of a heart attack.

It was still dark when at 4 a.m. on Election Day, Gravesend's Town Hall bell rang and rang summoning McKane's army of men. They were all prepared to come like minutemen at the sound of the bell, ready to defend the town and its illustrious leader. Meanwhile, a half hour later, the poll watchers gathered together at the home of William Gaynor, who lived at St. John's Place in Brooklyn. Colonel Alexander S. Bacon was well prepared to carry out his orders by handing McKane the injunction.

By this time, back at Gravesend, over 350 of McKane's "Keystone" style police gathered with clubs and bats. Voting was to begin at 6:33 a.m., but McKane made

GRAVESEND TOWN HALL. The site where the struggle between McKane's supporters and Colonel Bacon's men, the town hall was converted into a fire hall for Fire Engine Company 154 after Gravesend become part of Brooklyn. (Courtesy the Brooklyn Eagle.*)*

sure that everyone was there early, ready to face the poll-watching entourage. Across the street from the Town Hall, many of his men gathered at Hoerlin's Hotel drinking coffee and beer. McKane stood pompously in front of the Town Hall facing the north end of Gravesend Avenue where the Prospect Park and Coney Island Railroad ran. McKane knew that it would be from this direction that the "enemy" would arrive.

Finally, three carriages were spotted and as they drew nearer, a circle of McKane's men converged around them awaiting his word for action. While Colonel Bacon was preparing to descend from his carriage, McKane stepped up and said to him, "So you are here at last. You might as well understand that we don't want you here. Now get out!"

Colonel Bacon started to explain that he had with him an injunction signed by Justice Barnard and that he was ordered to hand it to him. McKane quickly replied, "I'll take no papers." He continued by stating that immortal phrase that would be echoed and re-echoed: "Injunctions don't go here!" The colonel insisted that he take the papers, and when he thrust the papers at him, touching his arm, someone in the McKane crowd shouted, "To hell with the Supreme Court!"

McKane's men immediately moved in, and when McKane stated, "Hustle that party out of here; run 'em in quick," all hell broke loose. A complete riot took place. Arms, legs, and fists flew in all directions. Bacon and his other men were knocked on their heads and were thrown into mud. McKane walked around gallantly saying, "Today we vote; tomorrow we talk."

Voting continued that day in the normal fashion with McKane's own men acting as poll watchers. "Martial law" was put into effect that day throughout the town. Anyone who did not have legitimate business in the town was thrown out. The trains and the roads were all guarded by McKane's men. Colonel Bacon and several of his men, including a clergyman, were taken to Coney Island's prison.

That afternoon, the *Brooklyn Eagle*'s headline read, "Injunctions Don't Go Here." The city fathers meanwhile were getting excited. Mayor David Boody, returning from voting, was told of the situation at Gravesend and remained dumbfounded. Gaynor, however, won the election with 93,774 votes. McKane only gave him 115 votes, while giving his opponent 3,506. People were urging Gaynor to get McKane punished for his actions. Gaynor agreed and assured the people that he would soon put an end to McKane's reign.

The reporters, meanwhile, gathered around McKane, and he began explaining to them his version of what occurred on Election Day:

> I'll tell you what occurred in a very few words. The Citizens of Gravesend are a quiet, law-abiding people, but they are capable, like all other good natured and honest souls, of getting stirred up when their rights are threatened. Now it was currently reported in Gravesend on the night before election day that Colonel Bacon and three hundred armed men were coming to town on election morning to make a violent

assault on the ballot boxes. This stirred up the people's souls and they got up early on Tuesday morning and naturally gathered around the town hall.

Well, when Bacon arrived in his carriage, the people naturally thought this was the vanguard of the armed force, and they gathered around the carriage. I was there, of course, as chief of police, and seeing the excitement around the carriage I walked over to find out what was going on. It was not entirely light at that hour in the morning, you know, and I didn't recognize Colonel Bacon. I asked him what he wanted. He replied that he had come in the interests of law and order and that he had an injunction, from the Supreme Court. But he didn't have any papers in his hand, and I saw no papers He said that another man had the injunction and called to someone to come up, saying, "Here's the man." But all this didn't interest me, and I turned around and walked off. That is all there is to this story so far as I personally am concerned.

But after I left, the crowd gathered around him [Bacon] and there was some little disturbance. I believe he and those with him created a disturbance around the polls, for the police arrested several of them, and I took them to police headquarters at Coney Island, where unfortunately a couple of them were locked up in cells. There was no necessity for locking them in cells; there was a room upstairs where they might have been lodged just as well. Afterwards I sent Judge Newton to look after them and he released them.

Now, that is the whole story of a small disturbance at the polls that has been distorted into simply an amazing sensation. As far as any Supreme Court injunction was concerned, no papers were served on me and I saw no papers of any kind. But see here, I find by the papers that without knowing about the injunction I unwittingly obeyed it to the letter.

One week had gone by after the "Gravesend Incident" and already the "natives" were restless. At Montague Street, people gathered at the Brooklyn Academy of Music. Plans were being made to punish "the Gravesend scoundrel." Suits for false arrest and the talk of prosecution didn't trouble McKane at all. When the caldron got hotter, McKane decided to take a vacation in Virginia. Being so self-assured, he announced his departure and left his address where he could be reached "if" an emergency were to occur.

While away on vacation, the court cited McKane for contempt of court for ignoring Judge Barnard's injunction. Jere Wernberg, who was a criminal lawyer, secured a warrant of arrest for McKane and several others of his men. McKane's emergency had occurred and he was now back. He avoided being imprisoned and fined for $250 once back, but soon enough he had to face the court.

McKane, being defended by his lawyer George W. Roderick, obtained at first an order from Justice Edgar M. Cullen to show cause why a stay pending appeal could not be granted after having been judged as guilty of contempt of court. This

CARTOON OF MCKANE'S IMPRISONMENT. The World *newspaper ran this political cartoon on December 27, 1893, expressing doubts on a conviction.*

case read, "Supreme Court, King's County. The people of the State of New York ex. ref. William J. Gaynor vs. John Y. McKane, Nicholas J. Johnson, Harlan Crandall, James H. Cropsey, Richard V. B. Newton and John Doe, policeman No. 11."

The official trial began on January 23, 1894. Gaynor and John T. Hinman, captain of the Gravesend police force, were just two of the witnesses who testified before the hearings. Special prosecutors named by the governor included Edward M. Shepard and Benjamin F. Tracy. Justice Willard Bartlett presided. When Edward Grout testified, he told how when McKane was told of the injunction he moved away and said, "I don't give a damn for all the judges and courts in the State of New York. You can go no further!"

Finally, the death knell sounded; the die was cast. McKane was convicted on 11 counts, including assault, conspiracy, contempt of court, aiding and abetting election officials in violation of the election law, misconduct of registry, and oppression. On February 19, 1894, the verdict was announced. While awaiting the announcement, McKane stood motionless yet a bit hopeful, thinking that someone, somewhere, might fix it all up. But poetic justice triumphed. For while the verdict of guilty was announced by Justice Bartlett, Justice Gaynor sat on equal par almost as if sharing in delivering the verdict. McKane, who by now had turned gray, lost all the red color in his face. He was sentenced to six years at the State Penitentiary at hard labor. As McKane was taken away from the courtroom on the third floor of Brooklyn's City Hall (now Borough Hall), Gaynor looked up and said, "God still reigns and the people are supreme."

McKane was taken to the Raymond Street Jail, where he remained until March 1, 1894, when he was taken to Sing Sing Prison. He was taken first by carriage across the Brooklyn Bridge and then to the train station for the trip to the prison. There, he remained depressed, alone, not wanting to see anyone. As prisoner number 119, he obeyed all rules and was released on April 30, 1898, on good behavior after having spent four years incarcerated.

McKane returned to his home in the Sheepshead Bay section of Gravesend. But all was different. Shortly after his imprisonment, the city fathers were victorious in getting Gravesend to become part of the City of Brooklyn. It was on April 26, 1894, that a bill was passed in the New York State legislature annexing Gravesend to the City of Brooklyn. And it was on May 3, 1894, that the town, as pursuant to chapter 449, laws of 1894, yielded its township. No longer would Gravesend rule in an autonomous fashion. Gravesend was no longer a town. From 1645 up until 1894, Gravesend governed itself. Now it would have to adhere to the rules and regulations of the City of Brooklyn.

McKane returned in poor health and went back to work selling life insurance. On August 10, 1899, while at the beach at Coney Island, he was stricken with paralysis. He was superintending the rebuilding of some of the homes that were

ESCORTED TO THE SENTENCING. *John McKane (left, handcuffed to officer) is seen here on February 19, 1894, as he walks to his trial at Brooklyn's City Hall. (Courtesy the James A. Kelly Local Historical Studies Institute.)*

destroyed as a result of a fire which broke out in West Brighton in May. Damages were estimated at nearly $800,000. He remained ill for about a week and then recovered and went back to business. A slight relapse occurred on August 28, 1899, but by Saturday, September 2, he was out at Coney Island—not knowing that this would be his last visit. Monday morning came and, not seeing her husband, Mrs. McKane went into the bedroom to call for him. It was about 6 a.m. when she went into the bedroom and found him unconscious. Immediately Doctors Hill and John A. McCorkie were summoned, and they succeeded in reviving McKane slightly. By 10 a.m., he was seized with a choking fit that grew worse. At 2 p.m., he lost consciousness again. On the evening of the September 5, McKane's family gathered around his bedside. Present were his wife; his two sons, George and Ira, with their wives; his sisters-in-law, Miss Nostrand and Mrs. Sumner; his brother-in-law, William Nostrand; his family physician, Dr. J.O.F. Hill; and two nurses. His 16-year-old daughter, Fannie, and his 90-year-old mother were kept out of the room.

McKane finally passed away after seemingly painless last moments. Dr. Hill described the cause of death as an embolism of the brain, which caused the paralysis. Other ailments which helped to aggravate the situation were Bright's disease, acute indigestion, and fatty degeneration of the heart and blood vessels.

McKane's wife became very ill an hour after his death, so Dr. Hill was recalled to the home. Funeral services were then planned to be held at the Methodist church at Sheepshead Bay.

From 10 a.m. on Sunday, September 10, until 3 p.m. in the afternoon, the body of John McKane lay in state at his residence. Over 1,000 people passed by the coffin to get a final look at the once powerful ruler of Gravesend.

His coffin was placed in the passageway between the front and back parlor of the home. The entire home was transformed into a veritable greenhouse. Flower arrangements were everywhere. The largest was a towering cross of roses donated by George W. Roderick, who was McKane's lawyer. A floral pillow at the head of the coffin read "Teacher." Other flowers came from the Order of Odd Fellows, the Franklin Masonic Lodge, the Thirty-Third Battalion of the Fire Department, the Robert F. Sutherland Association, the Seventh District Democratic Club, and the performers and employees of the Lawrence Dancing Pavilion. One of the biggest floral arrangements came from John Kavachis, a person for whom McKane had recently built a hotel on the island.

Several hundred people began to gather at the home around 2 p.m. for the procession from the home. Carriages were lined up for several blocks. Many distinguished citizens of the area arrived for the funeral. Councilmen Doyle and Francisco, Aldermen Keegan and Velton, Assemblymen Gallagher and Juengst, Magistrate J. Lott Nostrand, and Deputy Bridge Commissioner Murtha were all present.

The funeral procession began at 3 p.m. for the Greenwood Cemetery. There were three carriages filled with flowers. Alongside the hearse walked the pallbearers—S. Stryker Williamson, Michael J. Dady, George W. Roderick,

Benjamin Cohen, Henry Osborn, Augustus Friend, Alonzo Treadwell, and Conrad Studenbord. The Hebrew Benevolent Association, the Citizens' Association, and the Exempt Firemen were on hand, marching on foot behind the over-60 carriage cortege.

As they moved ahead, many citizens peered from the windows of their homes as the bells from all the churches of Gravesend tolled in unison. Many wept as the coffin was lowered into the ground, resting next to the place John McKane's son was buried. Originally, McKane was to be buried at the Gravesend Cemetery, for even today, one can see the ornate McKane Memorial, which was to be his at the cemetery. His well-attended funeral was proof enough, that even though he did wrong, people still loved and respected him. The years spent in jail, the humiliation he received, and the physical suffering he underwent, were all but enough punishment. McKane left no will, but people claimed that he left over $250,000 worth of property to his family.

McKane's passing can best be described by poet Alexander Pope when he wrote, "And you, brave Cabham to the latest breath, / Shall feel your ruling passion strong in death." McKane was gone. The Town of Gravesend no longer existed, and the city to which Gravesend had yielded had itself yielded on January 1, 1898, becoming the Borough of Brooklyn in the City of New York.

Although Gravesend did not exist as a town, people still referred to it as Gravesend. And as shall become evident, many positive changes were soon to take place as the nineteenth century gave birth to the "Century of Miracles."

THE JOHN Y. MCKANE ASSOCIATION, 1881. The members pose for this portrait in front of the Prospect Park Fair Ground and Race Course—better days for McKane's power and influence over Gravesend and Coney Island.

5. The Age of Progress

The "Gay Nineties" had ended and the era of municipal bureaucracy for Brooklyn began as its City Hall now became the Borough Hall. The politicos' choice for the first borough president was Edward M. Grout, who served from 1898 to 1901.

Since the opening of the Brooklyn Bridge in 1883, people came by the hundreds to Brooklyn's "tropical isle"—Coney Island. The nickel train and trolley ride now brought "the tired, the poor and huddled masses" to the refreshing shores of Gravesend. Strange and colorful shapes were now taking form as the hope for Coney's improvement was realized.

The first threat to Steeplechase Park came with the opening of Luna Park on May 2, 1903. The park was started by Fred Thompson and Skip Dundy, who, after working for George Tilyou at Steeplechase, decided to go into business for themselves. They purchased land from Captain Paul Boyton, who ran the Sea Lion Park. Luna Park was then built on the site where the Sea Lion Park once stood. Dundy suggested that this new park be named after his sister, Luna Dundy.

Nearly a quarter of a million electric lights were turned on the first evening. Over 40,000 persons visited the 22-acre park within two hours after its opening. Admission was 10¢. The initial cost for Luna was about $700,000, but expenses grew as the park was improved with new additions.

Luna Park featured the following attractions: the Streets of Delhi, Fire and Flames, Trip to the Moon, Twenty Thousand Leagues Under the Sea, Shoot the Chutes, the Scenic Railroad, the Circle Swing, Whirl the Whirl, the Infant Incubators, Sea on Land, the Faal Wedding, the Old Mill, the Miniature Railway, and the Laughing Show. Others amusements included the Three Ring Circus in Mid-Air, with the grandest aggregation of acts in the history of the tented arena; the Herbert Troupe, America's and Europe's wonderful flying return act; the Stickneys, the bareback, somersault, and high school equestrians; the Great Vinella and His Eleven Horses; the Spessardy's Bears; Will Hill, the high-wire artist; Dracula, the aerial contortionist; Zolas, the globe and spiral tower; Kelter,

FORE COURT OF LUNA PARK, C. 1905. Located on the north side of Surf Avenue, Luna Park opened in May 1903 and closed after a fire in 1949.

the swing and bending wire; Josie Ashton, the bareback rider; the Jennetts, the equilibrists; Francois, Du Crow, and Loranz; Zanzas, the breakaway ladder; Bonner, the educated horse; James Irwin, the head balancer; Rayno's 8 Wonderful Bull Dogs; the Plunging Elephants; and Dubar of India with his Working Elephants. Luna's many rides included the Tickler, the Bump-Bump, the Virginia Reed, and the Witching Waves.

Luna's lights and multi-colored buildings were so impressive that Maxim Gorki, a Russian novelist who had visited the park, noted the following:

> With the advent of night a fantastic city all of fire suddenly rises from the ocean into the sky. Thousands of ruddy sparks glimmer in the darkness, limping in fine, sensitive outline on the black background of the sky shapely towers of miraculous castles, palaces and temples. Golden gossamer threads tremble in the air. They intertwine in transparent flaming patterns, which flutter and melt away, in love with their own beauty mirrored in the waters. Fabulous beyond conceiving, ineffably beautiful, is this fiery scintillation.

There was also the baroque kaleidoscopic tower that changed color every second while the lighted spires, domes, and battlements were "not surpassed even by the stars." The people who visited Luna were also able to see an "Eskimo

LUNA PARK, 1923. A large crowd of onlookers are enjoying the acts in this mini-circus held in the park after a baby parade.

Village" and take a "Trip to the North Pole." The Japanese Tea Houses offered lovely Geisha girls as attendants at their "first class modern, up-to-date restaurant."

An era of great shows was introduced at Coney Island with Luna's many attractions. Mount Pelee, which "by electric appliance, water and pictorial effect" demonstrated the devastation wrought by the eruption in Martinique in 1902, and the Johnstown Flood, a re-creation of the tragic overflow of the Conemaugh and Stonycreek Rivers at the base of the Allegheny Mountains in 1889, were just two of the many shows at Luna Park. Nearly 1,000 people were employed by Luna to stage the Fire and Flames exhibit.

Luna Park was unique in many ways. It exhibited marionettes and featured cockroach racing. Dr. Martin Couney showed his "Preemies" at his baby incubator exhibit, which would often be visited by over 20,000 people on a summer Sunday. Dr. Couney's sideshow held the record for the longest running show (1903–1943) at Coney Island. Dr. Couney had in effect demonstrated the first baby incubator but not without first receiving some protest from the Brooklyn Society for the Prevention of Cruelty to Children. The protest eventually quieted down and by the time he retired in 1943, 7,500 babies were saved out of the 8,500 preemies he tried to save.

In the same year that Luna Park opened, fire swept across the island destroying the Coney Island Rescue Home. Heat again rose with the politicians' concerns over prostitution, as they met at Stauch's to discuss the situation. Inspector Robert Emmet Dooly kept order on the island. Nearly 30 people would be arrested on a number of accounts before noon on a weekend day. The accounts included but was not limited to the following: assault, stealing, indecent exposure (such as a man taking off his shirt in public on the beach), and prostitution.

Luna Park also had its rival, for on May 15, 1904, Dreamland, the "Gibraltar of the Amusement World," opened. Its "Ajax" white buildings glittered as over 1,000,000 lights were turned on. Costing over $3,500,000, Dreamland was renowned for its architectural splendor. The massive Dreamland Tower reached the heavens at 375 feet. It was the most conspicuous structure for miles around and could be seen at a distance of nearly 50 miles out at sea. At night the tower was illuminated by 10,000 electric lights. The tower was crowned with a huge spotlight, which acted as a beacon of welcome. Two elevators carried visitors to the top of the tower where they would view the scene of Dreamland's fairyland-type structures.

LUNA PARK, 1925. The Roller Coaster Ride was one of Luna Park's most popular attractions during its heyday.

ENTRANCE TO DREAMLAND. This extravagant piece of architecture served as the entry point into Dreamland for throngs of amusement seekers on Coney Island.

Senator William H. Reynolds was the principal investor in Dreamland, and he hired 2,000 skilled mechanics and carpenters needed to complete the amusement park. Dreamland boasted the magnificent Ballroom, which was completed in the Renaissance style. It was the largest ballroom in the world, having over 25,000 square feet for dancing. It was built over the ocean on the immense Iron Pier and was lit by 10,000 electric lights.

Dreamland featured Frank C. Bostock's Animal Show, which started at the Sea Beach Palace. Captain Bonavita and Colonel Joseph G. Ferrari performed with a group of 27 lions. Madame Morrelli brought on seven of her most treacherous specimens of leopards. Herman Weedom entertained with his motley group of lions, tigers, polar bears, hyenas, leopards, and dogs. Labelle Silica acted as an Algerian dancer and lion trainer.

Among the attractions at Dreamland was the "the Chilkoot Pass," a human bagatelle in which visitors were able to slide down through a labyrinth of obstacles landing in pockets having numbers. The one who got into the pocket with the highest number carried off the prize. Then, there was the Funny Room; the Fishing Pond, conducted by Andrew Mack; and the Venetian Building. The Venetian Building included the canals of Venice, which took the visitor through the most beautiful parts of the historic Italian city and displayed the famous Bridge of Sighs. The Coasting Through Switzerland attraction floated visitors past snow-capped Alps in a delightfully cool atmosphere.

Fighting the Flames was the most realistic reproduction done of a city fire, in which there were real flames and firemen. Leap the Frog Railroad scared many;

its two trains seemed certain to meet in collision, but unexpectedly one leaped over the other and traffic was not interrupted.

The park featured Santos Dumont's airship No. 9, which made frequent trips over the ocean offering an entire view of the island. The famous Shoot the Chutes ride was the largest of its kind. This ride would have two boats descending side by side splashing into a pool of water wetting the passengers inside the boat. A bit of old Nuremberg in the fifteenth century was reproduced at Dreamland's Midget Village, featuring over 300 "Lilliputians." An entire village built to the scale of the midgets was reproduced including a theater and circus, fire department, quaint houses, and a hotel. Mercy Lavinia Warren Bump Stratton, the 32-inch-tall widow of General Tom Thumb Stratton, was on hand at the village to entertain. Lavinia was a good friend of President Ulysses S. Grant, Napoleon III, and King Victor Emmanuel of Italy, among others. Other midgets at the village included Baron Magee and Count Magee. Baron Paucci, who stood 24 inches high, was also to be seen at Coney Island.

"The Greatest Aggregation of Educated Animals on Earth" performed at Professor Wormwood's Monkey Theater. E.D. Boyce's invention, the Submarine Boat, carried the passengers beneath the waters of the Atlantic, permitting them to view from the portholes fish, sharks, and other inhabitants of the deep. The Pompeian Building offered the "Fall of Pompeii." Under the direction of Messrs. Gates and Morange, Italian artists, it re-created the entire city of Pompeii, showing the eruption of Vesuvius in 79 A.D. Extraordinary electrical displays showed the burning of the city by the molten lava. To all appearances, real fire belched forth from the interior of the earth, and clouds of smoke obscured the sky, whence fell a terrific rain of ashes and rock.

Samuel W. Gumpertz, the owner of Dreamland, brought all types of freaks to Coney Island. There was the Human Fountain, who expelled water from his toes and fingers; the Fat Lady; the Tattooed Wonder; the Biggest Giant in History; and Zip, a sideshow hairy performer whose small Mohawk-style pin head joined in the freaky buffoonery. A tribe of Igorots shipped in by Gumpertz was the highlight of the "world of weirdos" at Coney Island. Warriors from French Somaliland attacked the island. Percilla, the "Monkey Girl" whose hair grew thickly over her entire body, attracted many a man. Emmitt Bejano, whose ichthyosis turned him into a gray scaly thing, was the Alligator Boy. Jane Barnell was the Bearded Lady, and Captain Fred Waters, by taking overdoses of silver nitrate, appeared as the Blue Man. Every type of freak came to Coney Island to amaze the innocent passersby: the Turtle Girl; the Human Auto Tire; the Human Ostrich; the Leopard Girl; Albert-Alberta, Half Man-Half Woman; and the Snake Dancer.

Angelo Siciliano was Coney Island's first strong man. Angelo was strong enough to hold a man in each of his hands and could tear two telephone books into shreds at the same time. Who knows, maybe it was the "pasta fagioli" that made him do it? His strength and his well-developed body won him the title as "the World's Most Perfectly Developed Man." Siciliano was commonly known as

CONEY ISLAND BOARDWALK, 1923. A large crowd of people are gathered in front of Stauch's on the Boardwalk.

Charles Atlas. William Lincoln Travis followed him as a strong man by performing at Professor Sam Wagner's World Circus Sideshow.

People could very easily escape such strangeness, and they often did by attending a number of cabarets and concert halls that furnished free entertainment. Some of them included Henderson's, Feltman's, Stauch's, the Auto, Maggie White's, Jack's, and Diamond Tony's, which employed male entertainers who performed in female garb.

Truly, Coney Island had now become the most popular resort and amusement area in the world ablaze with myriads of electric lights and filled with so many different kinds of amusement resorts that a single day was not enough for viewing them. Some visitors found it hard to comprehend that Coney Island was at one time a primitive collection of the rudest bathhouses and wooden hotels and shanty-like dance halls.

One of the truly interesting establishments was the Eden Musee. Here, many would come to see the outstanding wax representations. There was a gallery of waxen American presidents and a Chamber of Horrors; the Underground Chinatown exhibit scared many who walked passed the depressing atmosphere with its poor lighting. Among the famous people who were molded into wax were Charles Lindbergh; Gerald Chapman, the murderer; Leopold and Loeb; Charlie

Chaplin; Douglas Fairbanks; Mary Pickford; Bebe Daniels; Milton Sills; and Dorothy Gish. Unfortunately, a fire in 1928 melted the entire population at the Musee. The Winter Garden at the Eden Theatre was the scene of the Cinematograph. Music was provided at the theatre by the Royal Blue Hungarian Orchestra and the Royal Italian Orchestra. Admission was 25¢ and concerts began at 2:15 p.m.

William F. Mangels, the German-born amusement ride inventor, added many new rides at Coney Island. From 1902 to 1914, he operated a carousel. Mangels patented a new type of gearing for carousels in 1907, one year after he invented the Tickler, which was considered a fiendish ride. In 1914, he invented the famous ride called the Whip. He established the American Museum of Public Recreation at Coney Island in 1929. This museum contained photos and various articles tracing the development of hundreds of amusement devices. Failing to get financial support for the museum, he was forced to close it and sell the collection. Mangels was instrumental in planning the rides at the Palisades Amusement Park. In February 1958, at the age of 92, Mangels died in his home, located at 2825 Ocean Parkway.

Satan's hand touched the island at 4 a.m. on Sunday, July 28, 1907, and with his touch, fire broke out at the Cave of the Winds at Steeplechase Park. By 4:15 a.m., the fire had a good headway. Several watchmen in the building escaped and called in the alarm at 4:18. Three fire companies were at the park within moments of the alarm. Since Coney Island had a system of high-pressure saltwater mains, the fire engines did not connect with the regular water mains. The fans that made the breezes in the Cave of the Winds were at rest at 4:18, but a strong wind blew toward the southeast. Every piece of firefighting machinery between the island and Dean Street in Brooklyn was called in when Battalion Chief Rogers turned in a second, a third, and a fourth alarm. The fire grew worse and the winds blew the flames stronger every minute. The Cave of the Winds was eaten up within minutes. The Coney Island Post Office was gutted, but the mail was saved. The wind was so strong that Frederick Nana's Hotel at Surf Avenue and West Sixteenth Street, located across the street from the fire, was burned slightly.

Panic broke out and people were running to their stores, hotels, and businesses to save their safes and belongings. Since pianos were hard to come by, they were next to be saved. Frankfurter sellers allowed thousands and thousands of their "red hot" hot dogs to be eaten up by the engulfing flames as long as their cash registers were retrieved.

Michael Maginn, leader of a group of gypsies who had their quarters down by the oceanfront, ran amuck through the streets with great emotional upset, screaming and tearing at his beard. His tent went up in the fire and being an alarmist, he told everyone he met that he lost $10,000: Actually when the truth came out, it was closer to $10 that he lost.

The fire had now destroyed Steeplechase Park and was heading eastward crossing Tilyou's Walk. Everything that stood in front of its path was engulfed in flames since it was made of dry wood. August Wilson's hotel, the Belvedere on

Tilyou's Walk between the Bowery and the ocean, valued at $25,000, went up as quick as a match flares. So did Victor Olsen's $8,000 hotel. Axel Young's hotel, the Buono Brothers barbershop, the Ring-the-Cane Palace of Albert Lotto, the big $30,000 hotel of William Ferris, which had burned once before, were all now gone. Over 200 waiters at Stauch's hotel and dancing hall were lined up in a fire brigade adding water to the roof. Others removed armfuls of silverware.

Manager Buttling of Dreamland stood on the rooftop dressed in pink pajamas and a green bathrobe, waving his arms as he directed nearly 100 men to water down the entire park. Dr. Robert Hall, a fire department surgeon, came to the fire at the second alarm. Father Joseph Brophy, pastor of Our Lady of Solace Church, worked with the firemen's rigging. Father Grogan, the fire department chaplain, kept the people back and pulled the hose. By 7 a.m., the fire was under control and Father Brophy left and went to his church for Mass. Several people were hurt and were taken nearby to the Coney Island Hospital. Stauch's fireproof building had halted the terrifying inferno.

The following is a list of the places that burned and the amount of the losses: George C. Tilyou's Steeplechase Park, $1,000,000; Thomas Blythe, grocer, Surf Avenue, $6,000; William G. Ferris, hotel, Bowery and Kensington Walk, $30,000; Sam Freischman, hotel, Bowery and Oceanic Walk, $2,000; John McCullough, shooting gallery, Bowery between Oceanic and Kensington Walk, $400; Harry Koian, hotel and bathing pavilion, on the beach, $50,000; Louis K. Lent, concert hall, Bowery and Kensington Walk, $350,000; Arkenau Brothers, bathing pavilion and hotel, Tilyou's Walk and the beach, $60,000; George Hoch, hotel and bathing pavilion, on the beach between Seaside and Oceanic Walks, $30,000; August Wilson, hotel, Tilyou's Walk, $25,000; Louis Stauch, $20,000; Albert Buschman, hotel, Bowery and Oceanic Walks, $10,000; G. Scarana, Italian Restaurant, Oceanic Walk between the Bowery and the beach, $10,000; Heyman & Gould, dance hall, Bowery between Kensington and Oceanic Walks, $50,000; Mosely & Feucht, Drop the Dip Railway, Bowery between Kensington and Oceanic Walks, $50,000; Antonio Cilento, grocer, Surf Avenue, $5,000; Herman Wacke, Trocadero Hotel, Bowery and Oceanic Walk, $15,000; Tony Polakos, restaurant, Bowery between Oceanic and Seaside Walks, $10,000; Victor Olesen, hotel, Tilyou's Walk, $8,000; estate of Axel Young, hotel, Bowery, $7,000; Buono Brothers, barbers, Kensington Walk, $1,000; Albert Lotto, Tilyou's Walk, $2,000; Julius Weiss, pool and billiards, $1,500; Buint Benso, Bowery, between Oceanic and Kensington Walks, $5,000; and Joseph White, Rosenben Hotel, Seaside Walk, $2,000. Many of the places that were destroyed were uninsured, and therefore did not rebuild. One of the places that was uninsured was Steeplechase.

After the fire faded, reporters spoke to George Tilyou. "No, I didn't have one dollar in insurance. It is not so bad after all; nobody was killed. But one may die, I am told. That's the worst of it all." Tilyou continued as if he was the captain of a sunken ship by stating, "All my employees worked like heroes; they were heroes. It would have been real bad if several persons had been killed. But all this can be put up again. But I don't know when—don't know when." Shortly after the fire, however, Tilyou erected the new, all-weatherproof Steeplechase, which many continued to enjoy until the mid-1960s, when it was demolished.

Fire again wreaked havoc on the island a year later on July 8, 1907, destroying Pabst's Loop Hotel and Vanderveer's Hotel, which was located at Surf Avenue and West Fifth Street. Damage was estimated at about $200,000.

Satan's fiery hand struck again, this time, ironically enough, at Dreamland's exhibit Hell Gate. The fire began around 1:30 a.m. on Saturday, May 27, 1911. Apparently some men who were repairing the Hell Gate exhibit left a bucket of pitch on the roof, and when it fell, a spark from a nearby wire ignited the freshly tarred roof. The fire was reported shortly after 2 a.m. Fire engines throughout the entire city raced down Ocean Parkway, Coney Island Avenue, and Gravesend Avenue to the scene of the inferno.

Sergeant Klinck of the Coney Island Station immediately thought of the babies at the incubator exhibit. He, together with Dr. Fischal and Miss Grof, tried desperately to save the infants. Some were saved, but six of the infants died from suffocation.

The flames spread with such rapidity that Klinck could not get into the building again once leaving. The firemen had great difficulty containing the fire since the water-pumping stations were not working properly. The blaze was so great that to many it seemed to reflect the magnitude of the Chicago fire of 1871. New York

FIRE AT WHITNEY'S BATH, 1924. Many of the buildings and amusement rides on Coney Island fell victim to numerous fires over the years.

DREAMLAND TOWER. This 375-foot beacon to the park's attractions burned on May 27, 1911.

City's fireboats, the *Seth Low*, the *New Yorker*, and the *Zophar Mills*, were called in to help extinguish the fire that now had spread to Dreamland's steel pier and the Iron Pier. Nearly 400 men were at work that night fighting flames. The two ocean liners, the *Santa Anna* and the *La Lorraine* of the French Line, viewed the tragic fire several miles out at sea, which at first they thought to be an extravagant fire exhibit on the island.

The animals at Bostock's exhibit began howling at the top of their lungs as Captain Joseph Ferrari tried to reach them. Many of the animals were afraid, and soon they escaped running across Surf Avenue. Quickly people left their positions and climbed as quickly as possible to a nearby pole. Black Prince, the lion, came out of Dreamland's Creation ablaze with fire. He raced from there into the ride, Rocky Road to Dublin. Panic broke out and people and policemen alike ran for their lives, ducking the bullets that flew by. Black Prince was finally killed as he reached the top of the ride and motioned to leap on the crowd, which by this time had gathered below him.

The beautiful Dreamland Tower caught fire and collapsed at 2:40 a.m. "Why we were sitting on our front porch [1961 McDonald Avenue] the night Dreamland burned down and the tower was right at the very end of Gravesend Avenue. All of a sudden we saw it [the tower] topple over with a lot of sparks and red flames," remembered Miss Rae Johnson, a longtime resident of Gravesend and a descendent of both James Hubbard and Ferdinand Van Sicklen, who helped to settle the town.

At 3:10 a.m., the Iron Tower fell. Five minutes later the fire had spread as far west as Feltman's. After seeing the blaze spread, Deputy Fire Chief Dally declared that the fire threatened to become the worst that the island had ever experienced. The fire fanned both north and south and east and west. Samuel W. Gumpertz, the manager of Dreamland who had escaped the fire of 1907, gave the order that the animals were to be shot. Gumpertz stood over the ruins of his Dreamland, which to him seemed like a "nightmare." The devastating inferno had destroyed his $3,500,000 park, for which he was insured for only $500,000.

Ravaged in the fire were the following: Steubenbord's Restaurant, valued at $5,000; Abe Lenty's Dancing Pavilion, $50,000; Johnson's carousel and pavilion, $75,000; the Whirlwind Ride, $75,000; L.A. Thompson's Oriental Scenic Railway, $95,000; Pike's Peak Railway, $75,000; Stratton's Hotel, $60,000; Jolly's Hotel, $50,000; and Julius Frosin's Hotel, $50,000. The Galveston Flood and the El Dorado carousel were also gone.

As the Bible states that "the last shall be first and the first shall be last," so was it true for Dreamland. It was the last of three major amusement parks to be built, but it was the first to go, while Steeplechase being the first, was the longest to survive. All that was left of Dreamland were the fond memories and the song, "Meet Me Tonight in Dreamland." The City of New York purchased Dreamland's real estate for $1,800,000, and years later built the present New York Aquarium.

SITE OF THE OLD DREAMLAND PARK, 1923. The former site of Dreamland Park was used in 1923 as a municipal parking lot, and is now the site of the New York Aquarium.

Luna Park continued business and soon the ditty "Meet Me Tonight at Luna, Lena" was sung by the James J. Hogan's Band. Barron Collier, a businessman, took over Luna Park in 1912, selling it to a business syndicate in 1940. In 1944, it was sold again, and in the summer of that year, half of it was lost in a fire. Another fire in 1947 razed the old Trip to the Moon attraction. Luna's end came in 1949, when fire totally destroyed it for good. Today, the site where Luna Park once stood is occupied by the five tall multiple-dwellings named in its honor.

Coney Island continued, nonetheless, as Sigmund Freud noted when he visited it in 1909, as "a magnificent amusement area." Visitors to the island soon had a choice of three roller coasters. The Cyclone, 500 feet long and 86 feet at its highest point, was built in 1928 at a cost of $175,000. Charles A. Lindberg often enjoyed this roller coaster prior to his famous solo flight to Paris. The Thunderbolt and the Tornado were two of the other famous coaster rides.

Rides were constantly being introduced at the island. One of the more famous rides was the Caterpillar Ride. This celebrated amusement attraction was greatly enjoyed by young lovers. As it moved along a track, its hood would open and close at various intervals. Its closed hood drew criticism, however, from Mayor John F. Hylan in 1922, when he exclaimed, "I distinctly heard the sound of osculation [kissing]."

On October 1, 1921, Borough President Edward Riegelmann, of Brooklyn, drove the first stake for the Coney Island Boardwalk. The plans for the boardwalk were approved by the Board of Estimate and Apportionment on Friday, July 29, 1921. The length was to be 9,500 feet; width, 80 feet; and elevation, 14 feet. The boardwalk boasted some record-breaking statistics: 3,600,000 feet of treated timber, 120,000 tons of stone, and 1,700,000 cubic yards of sand-fill for the beach.

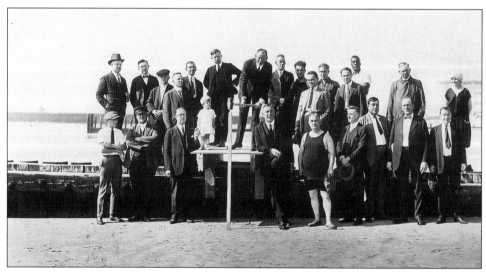

BOARDWALK CONSTRUCTION, 1921. Borough President Riegelmann is pictured here driving the first stake for the construction of the boardwalk on September 21, 1929.

CONSTRUCTION OF THE BOARDWALK, 1922. People still flocked to the beach in front of Martino's Bath despite the early construction work of the boardwalk.

Condemnation of buildings that were on the beach as well as securing the beach front as city property was necessary prior to the actual construction of the walk. On October 28, 1922, the first section of the boardwalk was opened between West Fifth Street and Ocean Parkway by Borough President Riegelmann. Other sections were gradually opened until the entire boardwalk was officially opened. The official boardwalk opening ceremony took place on May 15, 1923. Present for the historic occasion were Edward Riegelmann (the borough president of Brooklyn), Mayor John Hylan, Controller Charles L. Craig, and many other political, civic, and religious leaders of the city.

The day opened with a luncheon that was held at the Hotel Shelburne at Brighton Beach. General George A. Wingate was the chairman of the luncheon. Those who were present at the luncheon included Murray Hulbert, president of the Board of Aldermen; Controller Craig; Borough President Riegelmann; Borough President Maurice Connolly of Queens; Borough President Julius Miller of Manhattan; John H. McCooey; Jacob A. Livingston; the Reverend S. Parkes Cadman, for whom Cadman Plaza is named; the Reverend Walter Kirwin; and Rabbi Harry Halpern.

VISIT TO THE BOARDWALK, 1923. Mayor John F. Hylan and Borough President Riegelmann pose with a large crowd in front of Steeplechase Park on the early Boardwalk.

Following the luncheon, a flag was raised from the beach up a huge flagpole by Miss Adele McCooey, daughter of John McCooey. General Wingate acted as marshall of the parade, which took place down Surf Avenue. The parade passed the reviewing stands, which were placed on opposite sides of Surf Avenue. Mayor Hylan and Borough President Riegelmann greeted the many bands and marching groups that passed by.

Marching in the parade were the One Hundred First Cavalry, the Fourteenth Infantry, the One Hundred Fifth Artillery, the National Guards, the One Hundred Sixth Infantry, and the Police and the Fire Department bands. When the parade ended, the crowd gathered in front of the speakers' stand. General Wingate then introduced Father Kerwin, pastor of Our Lady of Solace Church at Coney Island, who pronounced an invocation. Mayor Hylan announced that New York was not the only city that would profit from the new walk, but that many other cities would also benefit. Borough President Riegelmann spoke, as did many of the guests assembled on the dais.

The day's celebration was capped by an extraordinary fireworks show. Despite the bad weather, thousands came that night to the island for the conclusion of the first day's ceremonies. At 8:45 p.m. that night, a parade was led down Surf Avenue by the Street Cleaning Department Band, followed by members of the Coney Island Board of Trade, members of the city's board of aldermen, city officials, and employees of the amusement parks with their bands. The mist settled on the island that night, but the people continued to dance on the boardwalk, which served as the largest ballroom in the world that evening.

Soon after, added facilities such as restrooms, gazebos, and benches were added to the walk. The boardwalk ran from the foot of Ocean Parkway to West Thirty-Seventh Street at the time of the opening day, but soon plans were under way to extend the walk. In the 1930s, Robert Moses, as parks commissioner, undertook the further extension of the boardwalk, extending it to Brighton Fifteenth Street by 1941.

The beautiful rolling chairs were a common sight on the walk from the 1920s until the 1950s, when service ended. Many enjoyed the gentle rolling of the chairs across the boardwalk as the sea breezes swept by. Of course, it was no pleasure for the person who was pushing the chair. As time went on, the boardwalk became known as the "Underwood Hotel." It was so nicknamed, since it provided a shelter to many and to others a place better than the backseat of a car.

THE COMFORT OF A ROLLING CHAIR, 1924. These two ladies are out enjoying a little "roll" on Coney Island's Boardwalk.

In 1929, the Half Moon Hotel opened for business. This 14-story building became a haven for many honeymooners. There, the newlywed couple could look out from their window and gaze at the moon reflected upon the Atlantic. In 1941, the hotel became the scene of a terrible accident; a man by the name of Abe Reles apparently sleepwalked right out of a window on the fourteenth floor. Many of his friends were saddened by his loss, while other friends of his showed what might be called a mysterious "Mona Lisa" smile the day of his death. Beautiful murals done by Eugene Zaikine were unveiled at the hotel in 1938. Unfortunately, the hotel was razed in the 1990s to make way for a new geriatric home.

Gravesend can boast of having been the site of the first "Hollywood" and thus the first film capital in America. Vitagraph Studios, then located at Avenue M and East Fourteenth Street near Locust Avenue, filmed many silent movies. Shortly after Thomas Edison's invention of the Kinetoscope, a man by the name of Albert E. Smith got together with his friend James Stuart Blackton and decided to start filming movies. Smith, who arrived in America in 1880, set up the Vitagraph Studios and used as his first headquarters the Morse Building, which was located at the corner of Beekman and Nassau Streets in Manhattan. In 1899, William T. Rock joined the studio. Albert Smith, the founder of the studio, served as president for a number of years. He later became treasurer and general manager, while William Rock served as president and J. Blackton served as vice president and secretary.

In 1903, construction began for the studios that were to be located at Avenue M and East Fourteenth Street in Gravesend. Additional buildings were constructed as time went on. In 1906, J. Blackton, the former newspaperman and exploiter of "chalk talks," produced *Humorous Phases of Funny Faces*, which was considered the first cartoon show. The new studios had all the modern equipment needed to

EAST TENTH STREET, 1924. *This view from Avenue M south on East Tenth Street was taken near the old Vitagraph Movie Studios site.*

produce silent films. Mercury vapor lights added in achieving the proper amount of lighting that was needed for indoors and for outdoors when there was overcast weather.

The Villain Still Pursued Her and *Julius Caesar* were two of the first silent movies produced at the Gravesend studio. The Vitagraph Studios attracted talent from across the nation. They even attracted a bearded, out-of-work revolutionary— Leon Trotsky. Trotsky, destined for a starring but ill-fated role in the Bolshevik takeover in Russia, served as a bit actor and part-time consultant. He starred in the movie *The Battle Cry of Peace*, with Norma Talmadge, Charles Richman, Ralph Ince, and Paul Scardon. The movie *The Life of Moses* was filmed basically indoors, but when it came time for the Israelites to cross the Red Sea, the beach of Coney Island provided the arid atmosphere and the Atlantic Ocean served as the sea. Other religious films included *The Illumination* and *Ben Hur*, which was shot at Manhattan Beach. Leo Delaney, the actor, starred in *Life's Yesterdays*, which came out on August 10, 1915. Ralph Ince produced *The Goddess* in 1915, which starred Anita Stewart and Carle Williams.

Life for the movie stars in the early days was tough. Some of the stars, for instance, had to build their own sets and organize their own wardrobe. Things got so bad that the stars began to strike. After the "White Rats" strikes were over, business returned to normal and stars returned to acting.

J. Blackton became notorious for his film making. In one movie, he arranged for actual servicemen from the Brooklyn Navy Yard to participate in a war film that was being produced near Mill Basin. Things were fine until the bombs that were exploding got out of control. Many men were seriously hurt and had to be rushed to the nearby Coney Island Hospital.

The film *Romeo and Juliet* starred Paul Panzer as Romeo, although Hughie Mack, the 300-plus-pound actor, really wanted the star role. Norma Talmadge, one of the famous Talmadge sisters (Constance, Natalie, and Norma), acted in *The Tale of Two Cities*. Actors such as William Shea, Vitagraph's oldest actor; Florence Turner; Maurice Costello; Adolph Menjou; Corrine Griffith; Lillian Walker; Charlie Chaplin; Fatty Arbuckle; Gary Cooper; Kate Price; Flora Finch; Mary Maurice; D. MacBride; John Bunny; Clara Kimball Young; Anita Stewart; Rodolpho Guglielmi (Rudolph Valentino); Mary Pickford; and Jean, the Vitagraph dog, all made motion pictures a reality.

Anita Stewart, who attended Public School 89 and later Erasmus High School, first acted in the film *The Wood Violet*. Wally Van acted in *Cutey's Waterloo*, *One Over on Cutey*, and *Cutey Tress Reporting*. Vitagraph was truly blessed with the genial and rotund comedian John Bunny. Bunny, who weighed in at 260 pounds, starred in such films as *Vanity Fair*, *Pickwick Papers*, *David Copperfield*, *Bachelor Bottons*, *A Cure of Pokeritus*, and *Bunny Attempts Suicide*. He became so popular that he won the title "King of the Coney Island Mardi Gras" in 1915. Shortly after that, he died at his home on Avenue G.

Roscoe C. (Fatty) Arbuckle joined Vitagraph in 1914 with the Mack Sennett Keystone Comedies. He starred with Buster Keaton in the movie *Coney Island*, which was mostly filmed at the beach and at Luna Park. Maurice George Washington Costello was known for having started the slow-motion style of acting that further enhanced the art of filmmaking. Clara Kimball Young, the once famous actress, performed in *Spirit of the Orient*, *Maid of Mandalay*, *Hindoo Charin*, and *Fellow Voyages*.

On several occasions people from Gravesend appeared in some of the films produced by Vitagraph. "Many a times we would get into the mob scenes when Vitagraph Studios shot movies," exclaimed Mrs. Anna Glorioso, a lifelong resident of Gravesend.

Faking newsreels and producing films of propaganda such as *Battle Cry of Peace* were all part of Vitagraph's struggle to survive and increase attendance at the local theaters. The producers wanted to create sensationalism as a kind of drawing card. Propaganda dealing with the evils of war and poverty were created to stir up the audience. However, things got bad when sound came to the films and the rumble of passing trains and trolleys were too much to cope with. In 1925, with the production of silent films flickering toward its end, the studios were sold for $15,000,000 to Warner Brothers. The "talkies" came to Gravesend and Brooklyn when Vitaphone, a subsidiary of Warner Brothers, started filming short-subject movies. It remained a movie center until 1939. The Kleig lights clicked off that year and stayed off for more than a decade. In the meanwhile, Warner Brothers continued to use the lab building to process its films.

In 1952, the National Broadcasting Company (NBC) rolled its television cameras into Gravesend, and the studios became active again. Since the studio had a tremendous built-in pool, it was a natural for the filming of the sinking of the *Titanic*. The studio also was renowned for its stage, which was considered the largest stage in the East. Mary Martin flew across the set in the movie *Peter Pan*, and Omar Shariff performed there when the movie *Mayerling* was being filmed.

Technicolor Corporation bought the property in 1957 and used one of the buildings to process black-and-white motion picture film. In 1962, the corporation rented the structures to Mayflower Scenic Company. Mayflower, which made sets for television, the stage, and the New York World's Fair, left the studios and Brooklyn in February 1964 for a new home in Long Island City, Queens. Kraft and Hallmark used the studio for their soap operas, such as *Bright Promises*, *Doctors*, and *Another World*. The *Perry Como Show*, the *Mitch Miller Show*, the *Alan King Show*, and the *Kraft Music Hall* were all produced, directed, and filmed at the studio.

In 1964, Yeshiva University of Manhattan purchased the property for its affiliated high schools in Brooklyn. After much work in renovating the structures, the girls' high school opened in September 1965 while the boys' high school commenced classes in September 1967. And so, movie and television production, another glorious and integral part of Gravesend's history, was lost!

Gravesend hosted many famous celebrities during the nineteenth century and well into the early part of the past twentieth century. The pleasures of Gravesend such as its oceanfront, fine hotels, and dinning were enjoyed by these noted people: movie stars and the rich and famous. Their beautiful remembrances in this, Brooklyn's most famous town, was often written about.

Well-known Gothic horror writer H.P. Lovecraft in his *Observations on Several Parts of North America* best described the village area of Gravesend during his visit in the early part of the twentieth century as follows:

> There were, of course, a sensible number of Dutch residents, as is manifest to this day in many family names. I had never seen Gravesend before, but came upon it without difficulty. Its present situation is very unfavourable, insomuch as the thickest part of it is buried beneath the trestles of an elevated railroad; but the number of buildings still standing is singularly large. Near on a dozen cottages in plain site date from before 1700, and not even the spreading of a vast colony of Italians can destroy the air of antiquity that hangs over the place. The Hicks-Platt (Lady Moody) house, a low cottage covered with thick ivy, was built in the time of Lady Moody; and within its walls the Holland governors, Willem Kieft and Petrus Stuyvesant, are known to have been entertained.

The Gravesend Town Hall, which served as a firehouse for the 154th Engine Company after Gravesend joined with the City of Brooklyn, was sold at auction on December 27, 1912, by Controller Prendergast for $200 to Harry Wolfson of 270 Madison Avenue. The 100-year-old, 76-foot-long structure met its end in January 1913, when it was torn down.

It wasn't too long before the elevated line was constructed down Gravesend Avenue, which was renamed McDonald Avenue on March 14, 1933. People of the community, unfortunately, petitioned the City to change the name from

GRAVESEND AVENUE, 1924. The elevated tracks appear above Gravesend Avenue, later renamed McDonald Avenue in 1933.

Gravesend, since they felt that its name was too morbid. "There is one cemetery at the north end of the avenue and another cemetery on the south end."

The name Gravesend was chosen by Lady Moody, who named it in honor of the Borough of Gravesend in England. The meaning of the word of Gravesend as recorded in the *Domesday Book* states that the town of Gravesend in England belonged to Odo, Bishop of Bayeux and called "Gravesham"; a name possibly derived from "graafham," the home of a reeve or bailiff of the lord of the manor. However, a more common theory for the derivation of Gravesend is that it came from the two Saxon words "grafes ende," meaning at the end of the grove. More likely, Gravesend means the end of the grove, and there is nothing morbid in that. Gravesend was never associated with a grave. But the people of Gravesend never bothered to research, and there was no historical society or heritage-minded organization to protest the name change, and so it was changed. The avenue was named after John F. McDonald, former chief clerk at the Surrogate Court who was the father of Miles F. McDonald, the then district attorney of King's County.

Where once corn stalks grew, iron and cement were now taking over as the Industrial Revolution seized the once tranquil community. Small dirt country lanes such as Johnson's, Ryder's, and Voorhees, which once served to connect one neighboring home with another, were now part of the expanding cement sidewalks and paved streets.

The beautiful Mill Pond, which stood in the Unionville section of Gravesend between Twenty-Seventh Avenue and Coney Island Creek near Cropsey Avenue, was filled in to make way for new homes, as were some of the creeks such as Broad's Creek, Leonard's Creek, Hog's Point Creek, Hubbard's Creek, and

GRAVESEND AVENUE, 1924. In this view looking north from Bay Parkway, the Washington Cemetery appears on the left.

Meandering Creek, which all wandered in a crisscross pattern throughout the southern section of Gravesend. The filling-in of these creeks is one of the primary reasons that some of the homes today suffer from periodic floodings every time a heavy rain occurs.

How many people today know that an old Indian pond was once located where Seth Low Park and School is located today, or that a beautiful natural spring was once situated between Avenue T and U in the center of Lake Street. These and many more of Mother Nature's wonders that once aided the earlier settlers, had disappeared.

Gravesend can date most of its home-building to the time of the 1920s. It was during this period that the City started a ten-year tax moratorium to encourage the further construction of residences. Where once the Brooklyn Jockey Club stood, streets were opened and beautiful villa-style homes with Spanish-tiled roofs and piazzas with stone urns were constructed. Today, this section on the east side is one of the most elegant sections of Gravesend. The area is patrolled with its own private police force, and basically only the rich or well-to-do can be found living there.

This affluent section of Gravesend has a sister community in the Manhattan Beach section. Located on such streets as Exeter, Beaumont, Oxford, Norfolk, Mackenzie, Langham, Kensington, and others, some of the loveliest homes in the area dot the plush, bucolic landscapes. This area of Manhattan Beach was created by Joseph P. Day, who established this private community with its own private beach.

Manhattan Beach soon became known for its entertainment and sports center. In addition to sports and swimming, in both ocean and pool, there was entertainment at the Rainbow Band Shell, which was later destroyed. Well-known figures such as Ozzie Nelson, Danny Kaye, Rudy Vallee, Xavier Cugat, Arthur Treacher, and the famous Sophie Tucker were just a few who entertained at the beach. The beautiful gates from the Gardens On Parade exhibit at the Botanical Gardens of the New York World's Fair of 1939 were taken to Manhattan Beach after the closing of the fair. Through those gates, many people passed as they entered Manhattan Beach.

Broadcasting by Henry Morgan and music by Benny Meroff and Rio Rita at the Rainbow Shell and Casino brought literally thousands to the shorefront to dance and make merry. The "Stop Hitler Campaign" in 1940 supported by Tallulah Bankhead and Helen Hayes, topped with a visit by Mayor La Guardia, added to the uniqueness of the famous beach resort.

By 1942, the merriment ended when the largest Coast Guard training facility in America was set up on Manhattan Beach, training 7,000 men and totaling 65,000 men. In 1946, the training facility was abandoned and a veterans' housing project was set up using the reconverted barracks for homes for war veterans and their families. On December 12, 1942, the United States Maritime Training Station formally opened, covering nearly 76 acres of the beach. It later served as a United States Air Force Base.

On January 30, 1964, Borough President Abe Stark of Brooklyn urged that the former 65-acre Air Force base at Manhattan Beach be selected as the site for the proposed Kingsborough Community College. "I think we should build on land presently available and appropriate for campus use, with a minimum of relocation and demolition problems. The Manhattan Beach site meets these requirements perfectly," stated Stark.

The Kingsborough Community College was approved "in principle" by the board of education on June 13, 1963. Since that date, the choice of the site for the educational facility was a source of considerable controversy, with various communities within the borough seeking to be its home. Stark called attention to the following important issues:

> [The new facility site] must be one that lends itself to considerable expansion without the necessity of encumbering too much of the open space for the campus use. . . . the projection of our city requirements for community college facilities show a need of eighteen thousand additional student accommodations by 1975. More than six thousand of these will be needed in Brooklyn. Again, Manhattan Beach more than any other appropriate college site in Brooklyn lends itself to this need for future expansion.

William F.R. Ballard, then chairman of the City Planning Commission, offered the following three alternate sites for the college: the Ebbets Field Urban Renewal Area; the area around Fulton Park, which is located at Chauncey and Fulton Streets and Stuyvesant and Lewis Avenues; and the Atlantic Terminal Renewal Area, which is in the general vicinity of the junction of Flatbush and Atlantic Avenues.

Common sense won out, and after the City applied to the federal government for conveyance of the Manhattan Beach property for public educational purposes, plans were drawn for the establishment of the college. Temporary structures were built and empty barracks were converted in time for the opening of the college in September 1964. A $100,000,000 campus was constructed with the first phase of construction, costing about $53,000,000, completed by the fall of the Bicentennial year—1976. The total project was completed in 1980s. The beautiful campus today hosts the beach that was once occupied by the famous Oriental Hotel.

Sheepshead Bay underwent many changes during this present century. The channels of the bay were being dredged and opened to receive larger boats. By 1913, the first large boat entered the bay. Party-boat fishing, still commonly enjoyed today, delighted many who would rise very early in the morning and rush to the piers not to miss the boat. The former presidential yacht of Theodore Roosevelt, which was used also by Franklin D. Roosevelt as secretary of the Navy, came often to Sheepshead Bay.

In 1934, under the order of Mayor Fiorello (Little Flower) La Guardia, work began on the widening of Emmons Avenue. Stores and other structures on the

WIDENING OF EMMONS AVENUE, 1934. Commissioner of Public Works Charles R. Ward is seen here starting to fill for the widening of the road.

south side of Emmons Avenue were removed. Nearly 11 piers built on an angle were constructed so as to accommodate the many fishing vessels that entered the bay. Much of Sheepshead Bay's beauty was lost, however, when the Belt Parkway was opened on June 29, 1940. The 34.9 miles of parkway costing $30,000,000 to construct was divided into three sections: Shore Parkway, which ran from Owl's Head to the vicinity of Woodhaven Boulevard; the Southern Parkway, incorporating the Sunrise Highway within the city limits; and the Cross Island Parkway north to Whitestone.

Robert Moses, who served as parks commissioner during the construction of the parkway, commented the following in the commemorative booklet: "We have gone back to the aboriginal Indian trails for the Belt Parkway. A glance will indicate that the red men were smarter than their successors in laying down lines of communication and travel." Despite the criticism of the parkway, it was a most needed facility. Master-builder Moses ingeniously created the parkway in such a way that it blended in with the natural surroundings. Horse riding was a pleasure to many, and a bridle path was added to the side of the parkway. Trees, plants, and shrubs of all kinds were not spared in landscaping the parkway. Where the Indians ran on forest paths, where the Dutch and English jogged on horseback, where cows drifted home for milking, now automobiles were ready to slip along, and

Nature would come to greet the tired city-dweller. Nearly 3,550 acres in 26 parks along the parkway were created for use by the traveler who might want to turn off the road for awhile and rest.

The opening ceremonies for the parkway began at 11 a.m. as the 4,000 guests assembled in a tent at Owl's Head Park in Bay Ridge. Airplanes from Mitchell Field and Floyd Bennett Airport saluted the guests by circling the site. Mayor La Guardia attended the ceremony and stated, "Frankness compels me to say that the message from the Mayor [at the time the parkway was proposed] asked that the matter be postponed. Now, let me tell you something. Twenty-four hours from now, people will be saying: 'How did we ever get along without it?' " Colonel Maurice E. Gilmore, regional director of the Public Works Administration commented, "I think it is nothing less than remarkable for Mr. Moses to have secured the record of performance he did."

Among the other guests and speakers were George V. Harvey, borough president of Queens; John Cashmore, borough president of Brooklyn; Stanley M. Isaacs, borough president of Manhattan; Newbold Morris, president of the New York City Council; Alan Johnson, general counsel of the Public Works Administration; and Harvey O. Schermerhorn, state commissioner of Highways, who saw the parkway as a "godsend for the country cousins of the residents of Brooklyn and Queens." The 2-mile stretch at Sheepshead Bay was not completed, however, until May 30, 1941. After the ceremonies were concluded and the ribbon was cut for the parkway, the group moved ahead as the caravan slowly rode the entire length of the highway.

Prior to highways being built, the rough dirt roads played havoc to the new automobile. Those that wished to race their cars attended the Sheepshead Bay Speedway. It was here that they would come to see the first car races. On

EAST NINETEENTH STREET, 1922. This photograph taken from Voorhies Avenue shows the muddy conditions early automobiles had to face.

EMMONS AVENUE, 1922. Before the general pavement of the area streets, early automobiles had to contend with a variety of road conditions.

September 17, 1917, thousands of people jammed the Sheepshead Bay Speedway to see Louis Chevrolet win the Auto Speed Championship. Some of the fastest drivers in the world flashed around the track at 100 miles per hour. Chevrolet won the Harkness $10,000 cup race that day and had to break the track record for the event to do so. It was a race of thrills and the vast crowd was on its toes every moment of the race. Chevrolet was given a hard battle for first honors. De Palma, who finished second, was close behind all the time. While Chevrolet was speeding around the track, something seemed to have leaped from the track, as he explained it, and hit him below the eye, raising a lump as big as an egg. Chevrolet crossed the winning line in his Frontenac, while Ira Vail came in third.

Car racing was not the only form of thrill seeking that the people enjoyed and the Town of Gravesend confronted. In 1883, residents feared that an old excursion boat, the *Express*, built in 1864, would be converted to a floating beer garden. They, of course, prevented it from happening, but epicureanism continued and matters grew worse. The Sheepshead Bay Property Owners Association complained in 1937, as did Coney Islanders years before, against nude bathers in the area. "Dancing and singing young men and women, forgetting modesty and bathing suits," the group said, "are wrecking the sleep and peace of homeowners." The secretary of the group complained further by stating that "This is a residential area and the appearance of these men and women on the streets does not add to the beauty of the section. . . . Liberty is a splendid thing, but this nude bathing is carrying it a bit too far."

One person was so enraged that he commented, "We ought to make those fellows who go bathing without shirts sit in a swamp where mosquitoes will eat them up for a few hours." He also wished that they be forced to "sit without shirts in freezing winter weather. . . . We're not Puritans, but when these hairy apes walk

S.S. SIMON AND JUDE CHURCH, 1923. This view looking west on Avenue T shows the construction of sewers in front of the church and rectory on the right.

on our streets and ride in our buses and subways, as well as going without bathing suits, something's got to be done about it. There are so many of those apes around on hot summer days, you'd think you were in the jungle instead of in a respectable section of Brooklyn." If the person continued talking, one could be sure that he would of stated that "Lady Moody must be turning in her grave by the actions of these apes."

Religious worship grew in Gravesend as both the Jewish and Catholic followers held services and renewed Lady Moody's privilege of religious freedom. The first Roman Catholic services to be held in the village area of Gravesend took place on Christmas Day, 1897. Father William A. Gardiner, newly assigned pastor of S.S. Simon and Jude Parish, offered the first Mass on the northwest corner of Avenue T and McDonald Avenue at Micacci's store.

Life was tough at first. Father Gardiner lived for awhile in a home owned by Mrs. Boyle at what is today 2000 McDonald Avenue. Sunday collections were small, bringing in about $6. After much work by the parishioners, a cornerstone was laid on October 23, 1898, for the first church. Volunteer labor with teams of horses dug the foundation for the religious edifice and it wasn't too long after that initial work that the country-style wooden structure was opened.

The parish grew as time went on, and plans called for the construction of a larger, modern church. On March 20, 1966, a new cornerstone was laid by Monsignor Joseph E. Egan, once pastor of the parish, and Father Stephen F. McGrail, who served as pastor at the time. The cornerstone was laid on the site where the old rectory stood. The new rectory, which was built first, now stands behind where the old church once stood. On Sunday, November 26, 1967, at 11 a.m., the new $1,200,000 church was opened and solemnly blessed by the then bishop of Brooklyn, the Most Reverend Bryan J. McEntegart.

The first of the Jewish services to take place in the village area of Gravesend was held at the home of Mrs. Esther Silver at 248 Van Sicklen Street in 1920. "My father, Tobias Cohn, got ten people together and started holding the first Jewish services in the community at the home where I live today, which at that time was 264 Van Sicklen Street," recalled Mrs. Silver. She further explained that since her father was a descendant of Aaron, Moses' brother, he was permitted to bless the entire congregation.

The area that Tobias Cohn first serviced was Quentin Road and Eighty-Sixth Street, on the north and south; and West Tenth Street and Homecrest Avenue on the west and east. Mrs. Silver's father, who at one time owned a toy factory in the Bay Ridge section of Brooklyn, transported the holy scrolls from a synagogue in Manhattan to Gravesend. Once in Gravesend, he placed them in an ark that was specially built for it. Services began in 1920, when Cohn arrived in Gravesend. On Saturdays, the singing and study of the Talmud, which is the philosophy of the Jewish faith, took place at Mrs. Silver's home.

"We then rented a store on McDonald Avenue for the services, once the congregation grew. After a while a synagogue was built on East Third Street between Avenue U and Avenue V known as the Congregation Beth El, which grew out of the services that were held in my home," remembered Mrs. Silver. As time went on, other congregations such as the Talmud Tifereth Israel were built.

During the 1950s, a fight broke out between neighbors in the village area of Gravesend. This fight was soon to be known as the "Battle of Lake Place." Since Lake Place was a private street, some of the homeowners felt that they could put up 3-foot-high fences across the unpaved road that stretched three blocks. The homeowners did in fact put the fences up so as to keep "the undesirable elements out." "Don't fence us in," cried the other homeowners whose access to their driveways was now being blocked by the fences. The battle went on for two years when finally the State Supreme Court upheld the anti-fence forces. Today, however, you will find that a fence does exist across Lake Place and Van Sicklen Street. Lake Place is one of the oldest streets in Gravesend. It was the first street that Lady Deborah Moody took to get to the village area once she arrived at Gravesend Bay. This tiny lane still runs for a few blocks from Van Sicklen Street near Corso Place to Eighty-Sixth Street. It once served as a main thoroughfare from Gravesend Bay and the mill to the village area. It was named for W.B. Lake, whose home bordered the lane. During the past hundreds of years, it was known as the Highway of West Meadows, Road to the Barrens to the Bay, and Gravesend Common Highway, among many others.

The beach at Coney Island became the scene of many strange habits. During the Depression, families would live on the beaches like nomadic tribes. Tents were set up and fires were started on the beach.

ROTARY SWEEPER, 1924. This early road sweeper was specially designed for snowy conditions on the Boardwalk.

The Iceberg Athletic Club and the Polar Bear Club were (and still today) seen during the cold winter months swimming in the frigid sea to the amusement of all. On New Year's Day, 1974, the Polar Bear Club, celebrating its 71st anniversary, raced into the cold Atlantic singing "Auld Lang Syne." The Polar Bear Club, was founded in 1903 by the late Bernard MacFadden. One of the former members of the club was a woman in her seventies. She joined the club in 1965, when the club was opened to women. The following poem sums up her reasons for being a Polar Bear.

> I fell into the water when I was a kid.
> On a frozen ford in Sweden testing my skating skill
> Since then I've been addicted, at heart a Polar Bear;
> With Polar Bears in Stockholm, I swam all winter there.
> And now I'm a really old lady
> But very young at heart—
> I swim in Coney Island, among the Polar Bears.

The Iceberg Athletic Club was founded in 1918 by Detective George O'Connor, who was long associated with the Missing Persons Bureau. O'Connor served as president until 1955, when his death introduced Doctor David Cory as president. Dr. Cory became a member of the Iceberg Club in 1938. He once stated that "the two aims of the club are first, all year-round swimming and second, sociability in the great outdoors." The club has 24 active members and has had at least six cases where they have saved people from drowning. Many members today are senior citizens and continue to venture into the chilly January Atlantic. One of their former most famous members included John Merel, who swam the Panama Canal. When asked the coldest temperature the club went swimming in, Dr. Cory replied, "Land temperature or water temperature? . . . Six degrees land and twenty-eight degrees water, since salt water freezes at twenty-seven degrees."

The "hot dog" industry continued to grow at Coney Island. On July 23, 1939, Coney Island celebrated "Hot Dog Day." Comedian Milton Berle served as master of ceremonies and stated on that occasion, "Let our slogan be 'E Pluribus Hot Dog.'"

Contests of all types were held at Coney Island. In 1942, a National Bathing Beauty Contest was held. The "Most Beautiful Grandmother Contest" in bathing suits was another memorable event that got much applause from the more mature male audience. Kissing marathons, the longest of which lasted three hours, occurred at Luna Park in 1933. Today, some of the contests that still are held at Coney are the Annual Twins Convention Contest, the Little Miss Pigtail Contest, and the annual Baby Day Contest.

BABY PARADE, 1923. Ruth Willett won second place in a baby parade celebrating the opening of the Boardwalk on May 17, 1923.

Coney Island did not escape politics nor the underworld as the century turned. Corruption continued to flourish at the island. Frankie Yale, who "stole from the rich to give to the poor," protected the local industry at Coney Island. He founded the Harvard Inn in 1916, and his chief bartender and bouncer was none other than Al Capone.

Mysticism played a part in Coney Island's history, and even today one can still see the last remnants of the gypsy tea readers, whose side street establishments, richly ornamented in red velvet drapes, draw the poor, superstitious passerby.

During 1939 and 1940, the New York World's Fair was held at Flushing Meadows, bringing with it new amusement ideas, such as the famous Parachute Jump. This famous ride was operated at the fair by the Safe Parachute Jump Company and was sponsored by the Life Savers Candy Company. During the combined two years at the fair, it brought in an estimated $358,250. During the fair, some of the daring riders on the jump included Gypsy Rose Lee, Abbott and Costello, and Bert Lahr. A marriage ceremony was performed during the descent of the parachutes on one occasion. The minister was in the center jump, while the two lovebirds quietly descended alongside him. Professor Arthur Konop of Brooklyn recalls being stuck on the jump as a young child at the fair, "We were up for over thirty minutes and from below they told us to relax. We were nearly two-thirds the way up when we got stuck. I can remember how the chute kept swaying back and forth with the wind." After the fair closed, the $750,000 ride, which would cost at least twice that much if built today, came to Coney Island. Reaching the heavens at 250 feet, the new ride began operating for Steeplechase Park in 1941.

THE PARACHUTE JUMP. The very symbol of Coney Island, this popular and memorable amusement ride is a New York City Landmark and is listed on the National Register of Historic Places.

CONEY ISLAND'S LIFEGUARDS, 1923. Borough President Riegelmann and other city officials pose with these lifeguards on September 12, 1923.

Although Charles Feltman was considered the first pioneer for Coney Island improvement, a later more outspoken pioneer emerged. As parks commissioner, Robert Moses, who later became the chairman of the Triborough Bridge and Tunnel Authority and president of the 1964–65 New York World's Fair, pledged his administration to abolishing the ballyhoo and strange wallahs at Coney Island. Since a law was passed in 1938 allowing the Parks Department to control the beach and boardwalk, Moses was ready and able to do so. Rubbish cans were placed on the beach and the boardwalk in order to alleviate the garbage build-up.

By the 1940s, the beach was so densely packed with crowds of people that Moses exclaimed with great distaste that the beach afforded its bathers each less than the 16 square feet required for a coffin. Moses wanted to get rid of the small wooden rides and exhibits that gave a cheap atmosphere to the island. His aim was to capitalize on the beach and the oceanfront: "More and more people are interested in the healthy, outdoor bathing-type of beach like Jones Beach, rather than in the mechanical-gadget resort like Coney Island. . . . The important thing is not to proceed in the mistaken belief that it can be revived. There must be a new and very different resort established in its place."

Under Moses's aegis, 7 new lifeguard stations were set up, 16 first aid stations were built, and many new drinking fountains came into existence. New comfort stations were also constructed to serve the uneasy bather. Redecking of the boardwalk took place as well as the realignment of a section of it, which was swerved. The beach was then extended by the addition of new, clean, white sand.

On October 24, 1954, ground was broken on the site where the beautiful Dreamland Park once stood for the erection of the new aquarium. The old aquarium stood in Battery Park until 1941, when construction of the Battery Tunnel forced it to close down. Soon after, the old aquarium was closed and land was purchased at Coney Island for the future aquarium.

This new aquarium, officially dedicated on June 5, 1957, was actually the second aquarium to be housed at Coney Island. During the 1880s, the Seaside Aquarium operated on the island. However, this aquarium ran unsuccessfully. The malodorous aquarium was forced to close when attendance dropped. The Aquarium at Coney Island was, as were many projects in New York City, the work of Robert Moses. In his book *Public Works: A Dangerous Trade* (1969), Moses speaks frankly about the new aquarium.

> Skepticism was manifested by zoo directors when I strongly urged that the Aquarium be moved to Coney Island from the sunken gas tank at the Battery, with its nostalgic fortress, Jenny Lind, immigration memories, and the dismal fish exhibits. Coney Island, it is true, had unpleasant seaside-circus associations and a bad name. I pointed out that this location was a natural, that the slums would disappear, that the community would become residential, that access would improve, and that there would be plenty of room for expansion and development of research as well as exhibition. This move was almost defeated, but we prevailed, and today even the most voluble of the old skeptics admits that we were right and that our logic was sound.
>
> Recently the Aquarium has acquired a fine new laboratory, which has greatly increased its usefulness in scientific research as well as exhibition, and the process of converting Coney Island to residence and recreation as distinguished from honky-tonk has been accelerated. The potentialities in this field are endless and fascinating.
>
> Tall apartments have grown up close to the Aquarium, which must be expanded to the west, probably by private donations, to meet the rising demands of enthusiastic visitors, especially school children. The cheap seaside catchpenny amusement shacks rented to itinerant showmen by absentee landlords still line Surf Avenue. Obviously the future of Coney Island inside the boardwalk and beach is residential, with the amusement area narrowly confined. A Tivoli on the Copenhagen model is not in the cards—too expensive and too refined for the rough element, which wants crude sideshows, shills, and barkers. The old seaside slum Coney Island is an empty shell. It may go on for a while, but the handwriting is on the wall.

Planned in the 1940s as the Oceanarium, the New York Aquarium today is host to many New York City visitors. The Osborn Laboratories of Marine Science, started in 1965 as part of the aquarium, continues further study of marine life. Odd and unique species of fish can be seen at the aquarium, which is considered one of the nation's best.

Alex, a 13-foot, 2,000-pound performing whale, and Olie, a 6-foot, female, white-sided dolphin, thrilled many spectators by their aquatic performances, as did Pete the Acrobatic Penguin, performing acrobatic feats while many laughed at his funny wiggle walk. There was also Francis, the 15-foot Beluga white whale, who for many months had the then aquarium director, Dr. James A. Oliver, and many others wondering whether or not she was pregnant. Francis, although a female, was named after an Indian whaler who helped capture her in 1967 at Seal River in Manitoba, Canada. It was finally discovered, however, too late, that she was truly pregnant. Francis died about 6:35 p.m. on May 25, 1974, of poisoning or toxemia which had been detected a week before. She was treated for it and seemed to be getting better, but the toxemia resulted from the death of her fetus, which had been dead for nearly a week. Francis was at the time the only white whale in captivity. All that is left of her are fond memories.

Injured whales, which at times are washed ashore at Coney Island, are treated at the aquarium, as are many other forms of marine life. The aquarium continues today to both educate the children and lovers of aquatic life, and it cares for and maintains the creatures from the deep sea.

In 1972 plans called for the destruction of the 46-year-old Cyclone roller coaster ride. On its site would, have been built a trout stream complete with fish. The Gravesend Historical Society prudently made application to the New York City Landmarks Preservation Commission to have the Cyclone declared a landmark. Today, this world-famous ride enjoys that status.

On June 12, 1963, plans were announced by Borough President Stark to commence immediate construction of two parking fields and an indoor skating rink, which would serve also as a convention center at Coney Island. "This is a beginning," Stark said. "I foresee added amusement areas and motels being built, thereby bringing about more prosperity for Coney Island and inspiring the refurbishing of existing facilities." Demolition began and some 500 people living in rooming houses scheduled to be torn down were moved by the Department of Relocation. Today, the beautiful ice skating rink is named in honor of Abe Stark.

But this was just a start in the development and improvement of Coney Island. Whatever happened to the plan which the Coney Island Chamber of Commerce drew up in 1965? Their $6,500,000 plan called for the development of the former Steeplechase Park. Released on December 3, 1965, the plan envisaged the construction of new oceanfront facilities including cabana-type structures atop lockers and showers, with a center sun deck area, picnic grounds, and parking for at least 1,000 additional cars on the 12.5-acre site. This plan was never realized. However, today, the former site of Steeplechase Park is the new home of the New York Mets' new 6,500-seat stadium for their farm team, the Brooklyn Cyclones.

A novel feature of that proposal called for the construction of a band shell for summer concerts at the end of the existing 1,200-foot pier, which extends into the ocean from the boardwalk at West Seventeenth Street. The plan was submitted to then Borough President Stark, who had been urging the creation of such a facility. He announced that he would communicate with then Secretary Stewart L. Udall of the United States Department of the Interior and invite him for a personal inspection of Coney Island's recreational needs and opportunities. Stark further stated at the time that as soon as the plan was worked out in more detail, he would see that it got the attention of the City Planning Commission, the Board of Estimate, and the Parks Department. But the attention was not obtained.

Where music was to have been piped by loudspeakers from the bandshell for the enjoyment of the bathers, the loud "cha-cha-cha" sound of music from a radio can be heard booming from the pier today while the Spanish-speaking fishermen draw up their cages filled with the polluted crabs. Many complain about Coney Island's shabby look. Its slums, dirty streets, and low-class hotels where hookers, pimps, and addicts form a coterie of unwanted souls. This is bad enough, but a greater problem is the way that real estate developers have destroyed the natural beauty of Coney Island. No thought has gone into the development of the high rises with relationship to aesthetic value.

On land that was at one time common land, developers made their money and created huge, 20-story buildings, which blocked out the view of the ocean from other Brooklynites who were at one time able to see it from their second-story windows. Common sense in planning would naturally have called for the tall buildings to be built further in from the shore, with small buildings near the shore. The further inshore one travels, the taller the buildings should be, thus enabling all to take advantage of both the sight and the breezes the ocean affords.

When told that their homes were condemned as part of "urban renewal," in the 1960s, the Italian homeowners got together and protested. The section that was in question was a small area of homes near West Sixteenth Street. Many of the people of this area could not understand how, after living in their homes all of their lives, fixing, repairing, and planting tomatoes in their yards, that now they were being told to move. Of course, once the homes came down, the high rises went up. The western-most end of Coney Island, Sea Gate, was left alone. Sea Gate is a private community of individuals who pay double taxes for the mere exclusivity of living in a private gated community on the western tip of Long Island. Until 1928, when he abandoned it, this area served as Governor Alfred E. Smith's summer residence.

The developers of housing at Coney Island and Brighton Beach constantly searched for property to acquire in order to build. One of the major developers was Fred C. Trump. In May 1973, the Brooklyn Supreme Court halted one of his projects. Trump was planning to fill in Coney Island Creek without authorization by the State Department of Environmental Conservation.

A nice piece of real estate was created when, on the evening of February 26, 1973, the century-old Bushman Bath Houses were destroyed. More than 30

ANDREW AST JR.'S HOTEL, 1923. Now the site of Trump Village, this hotel was once located on Sheepshead Bay Road.

pieces of fire apparatus and 120 firemen were summoned by three alarms to fight the blaze, which began at 10:30 p.m. and threatened Stack's Baths. Stack's was saved, but where Bushman's once stood, a lonely piece of land was left.

The latest addition to what is left of the amusement world at Coney Island, now that Steeplechase is gone, is Astroland. It is basically the main center today of the children's rides. Many of the concessionaires at Coney Island were pessimistic about the future of the island. Fred Moran, former owner of the recently demolished Thunderbolt roller coaster ride, was not. Opposed to the way Robert Moses viewed the amusement world at Coney, Moran felt that many people enjoy the "mechanical gadget resort." Unfortunately, almost like a curse, the "mechanical gadget resort" continues, never getting any better, but always seeming to get worse as the years pass. The odor of frying oil, the strange-colored shacks, and weird mystical symbols next to the painted hand of a gypsy palm reader all lend to the iniquitous and saddening condition of what was once "the Amusement Land of the World." Conditions did improve, however. High-intensity street lighting on the island was started on Mermaid Avenue when Mayor John Lindsay turned the lights on for the first time on November 3, 1972. Borough President Sebastian Leone of Brooklyn asked the City Planning Commission to appropriate $150,000 of the 1973–1974 capital budget funds for

STILLWELL AVENUE, 1918. These children are pictured on Stillwell Avenue in a view looking south toward Surf Avenue from Neptune Avenue.

the construction of a band shell on the 12.3 acres of Sea Side Park. The band shell, today, is the center of many musical concerts and performances

Sheepshead Bay had suffered much. Its fishing industry and seafood restaurants were vanishing and during the 1960s apartment dwellings grew by the dozens, thus destroying the seaport atmosphere. The community, however, protested and a special Sheepshead Bay zoning district was created. The City Planning Commission declared itself on record as wanting to "Preserve and upgrade the unique waterfront recreation and commercial neighborhood while stimulating appropriate new commercial and residential development in 1973." The provisions called for public plazas with lighting, pedestrian walks, and sitting areas. Borough President Leone stated on October 19, 1972, that Sheepshead Bay was "one of the most precious natural beauty resources left in the state. . . . the area never won any medals for its apartment houses, and I don't think it ever will."

On October 6, 1973, the Board of Estimate of the City of New York approved the special zoning district. Leone enthusiastically reported the following:

> I am delighted to announce Board of Estimate approval of a special zoning district for Sheepshead Bay which is truly one of the City's most interesting and beautiful areas. . . . This special district was created to preserve and improve the unique qualities which make Sheepshead Bay the highly desirable residential area that it is. What we have done is to

make certain that the area's salty charm will be retained by setting strict standards for new businesses and new housing alike. New commercial developments in the special district will be restricted to service, retail, amusement and boating activities that fit in with the area's special character. The height of most new business establishments will be restricted to two-story buildings while new housing will be subject to certain design requirements and limited to a maximum of seven stories in height.

The new district was made up of a major portion of the 20-block strip of the Shore Parkway, renamed Leif Erickson Drive, between Sheepshead Bay Road and Knapp Street. Emmons Avenue, the major thoroughfare in the area, forms the spine of the rectangular strip. Also included are the ten docks on the bay side of Emmons Avenue, which are used by commercial and charter fishing boat owners, along with related businesses and restaurants. Lundy's Restaurant, which laid abandoned for many years, has been renovated and serves the public proudly today. A sacred Holocaust Memorial Park was erected during the mid-1990s in Sheepshead Bay at Emmons Avenue and Shore Boulevard.

The Age of Progress during the 1970s took the form of destruction. The old Reuger House was demolished. However, in the summer of 1974, the community of Sheepshead Bay honored one of its own. The mall section of Bill Brown Square at the intersection of Sheepshead Bay Road, East Seventeenth Street, and Jerome Avenue was named the Vince Lombardi Mall, named after the famed coach of the Green Bay Packers who grew up in Sheepshead Bay.

Gravesend had come a long way from the tranquil days of the nineteenth century. The town had been part of the greater City of New York for over 100 years and had now come of age.

6. THE GREENING OF GRAVESEND

On December 17, 1973, the world turned to glass. An overnight storm brought snow and freezing rain, which in the dark hours before dawn transformed the metropolitan area into an ice palace. Temperatures remained below the freezing point the next two days preserving the crystalline shapes that glistened in the clear blue sky.

As snow annually covers the dirt and grime of the city with a white carpet, muffling the sounds and softening the sights of the urban landscape, this ice phenomenon of 1973 turned the city into a glittering fairyland. Old timers exclaimed that they had never seen anything quite like this frozen fantasia, which turned ordinary trees into ice sculptures. The trees took on new form as they talked in a continuing dialogue of "tinkles," while giving off the colors of the spectrum from long-frozen appendages.

Passing the sign proclaiming "Gravesend Neck Road" adorned with its very own and individual "ice art," the residents braved their way through this Winter Wonderland to the cemetery. Almost gliding across this natural ice rink were descendants of the settlers of this town, some whose remains lay only feet below the new layer of glass. Hand in hand with them for support walked the present-day inhabitants of the community, many of whom came as immigrants to these shores, or the sons and daughters of those who left the troubled and uncertain life of Europe to settle here. From ages 8 to 80, they came in this small improbable parade through Gravesend Cemetery on December 19, 1973.

What they came to mark in this ritual was the 330th anniversary of the founding of the Town of Gravesend. The new flagpole erected in the southern corner of the cemetery only days before was covered with a sheet of ice that had to be chipped away so that the rope could be free to perform its function of the day: to raise for the first time the new town flag of Gravesend. The simple heraldic banner depicts in the colors of Lady Moody and New Amsterdam, the central symbol of the town, the four original squares. Dr. Joseph Palisi, borough historian of Brooklyn,

GRAVESEND CEMETERY, 1935. Restoration work by the WPA of the Gravesend Cemetery was nearly completed when this photograph was taken on December 13, 1935.

and State Senator Donald Halperin slowly raised the flag above the town as the crowd and onlookers from nearby homes watched in silence. As the new town flag reached its summit, the applause of the onlookers joined the tinkling from the trees in breaking the quiet of this ancient burial ground. Only a matter of feet away, one observer noted, may rest Lady Moody herself, her name and her deeds not forgotten over three and a quarter centuries after her death.

This task accomplished, the hearty group made their way through the cemetery to the Gravesend School across the street for the official ceremonies. Walking to the school, Senator Halperin noted jokingly that he had proposed the renaming of Coney Island Hospital as "Gravesend Hospital," and couldn't understand some people's objections to this.

This occasion marked an important milestone in Gravesend's history. But it also marked the culmination of a long labor that resulted in the creation of the Gravesend Historical Society.

The ice was a hazard for those walking through the Gravesend Cemetery that day; however, only a little over one year before the obstacles in their path would have been far greater even in the best of weather. For the Gravesend Cemetery, the oldest and, at 1.6 acres, the smallest city cemetery, had been for years a dumping ground, a playground for vandals, an eyesore to the community, a disgrace to the living, and a desecration of the deceased of Gravesend. Toppled and cracked headstones, garbage, wrecked autos, and piles of filth were scattered throughout the grounds. At night the cemetery was a haunt of vandals and vagrants. In addition the only two identifying markers to this historic cemetery, which contains the graves of Indians and Revolutionary War soldiers, could barely be seen amidst the thick, jungle-like growth of weeds and underbrush that obscured all but the garbage. The two signs even proved incorrect. One, erected in 1938 by the New York State Education Department, states that Lady

145

Moody had founded the town along with her English Quakers. The followers were, of course, not Quakers, but Anabaptists. The other sign proclaimed that the cemetery was under the jurisdiction of the president of the Borough of Brooklyn.

A headline in the *Eagle* of July 22, 1917, states "Seek Fund to Preserve Old Gravesend Cemetery." The article reports that most of the historic and artistic headstones of the cemetery "were half fallen and the inscription on them made indecipherable by the action of time and the elements." William B. Lake, one of the descendants, was disturbed by this and was quoted in the article as follows:

> I am of the tenth year generation of one of the founders of Gravesend, and am proud to do anything to help sustain the memory of the original settlers. When I found that the town's "God's acre" was likely to fall into disuse and decay, I made up my mind that something should be done and I did what I could, that's all.

The article also noted that "Mr. Lake thinks that public sentiment might be roused through the *Eagle* which would result in the raising of money to properly enclose this historic burying ground and insure its preservation. At present there is no fund whatever for this purpose."

Then, in 1935, the *Eagle* again reports, "Five Trustees Sworn for Ancient Burial Plot of Gravesend Descendants of Borough's Oldest Families to Be Guardians of Tiny Plot." The story, dated June 20, 1935, reveals that five descendants were appointed by Mayor La Guardia and sworn in by Justice William F. Hagarty of the Appellate Division "to perpetuate and preserve Gravesend Cemetery." The newspaper reported the following:

> The ceremony, which took place in Borough President Ingersoll's office, linked the dim and distant past, when Brooklyn's pioneers were laid to rest more than 300 years ago, with the present moment. The trustees who used to have supervision of the care and maintenance of the cemetery have long since passed away and modern vandals seeking perhaps to link old Brooklyn history to new dollars, have carried away some of the oldest legible tombstones.

The Cemetery, at Gravesend Avenue (now McDonald Avenue) and Gravesend Neck Road, is owned by the City. It was a public property of the Town of Gravesend, which later became part of the City of Brooklyn. President Ingersoll told the new trustees that the restoration of the old cemetery to a state of order and dignity was in keeping, as a matter of public importance, to the preservation of the old Stone House and other spots of historic interest. Ingersoll also hastened plans to have a fence built around it. Workmen raised fallen tombstones and removed debris and weeds that had accumulated through years of neglect.

As when Justice Hagarty had administered the oath of office to five trustees, he said, "I can tell, as I look into your faces, that this important work has been placed in capable hands." The new trustees were Harry Bennett, William E. Johnson, Howard W. Voorhies, Fredric H. Ryder, and Wheeler N. Voorhees.

In 1955, an article in the *Sunday News* on January 30 proclaimed in a headline, "Comfort to Come to Old Cemetery." The article told how the City had undertaken to make new improvements on its cemeteries and a photograph showed cemetery caretaker John P. Vuzzo repairing an old tombstone. It was during the 1935 cleanup that a small brick caretaker's house was erected by the WPA in the northeast corner of the cemetery on Gravesend Neck Road.

In 1972, the 20-odd-year cycle came around as the grounds were again in deplorable shape. The caretaker's house was long since abandoned to squatters and rats. Having discovered this background, I sought to find a means of having the cemetery restored. It soon became apparent that there were no established mechanisms or institutions within the community to undertake the clean up. Most of the original descendants had long since passed away. Ironically, many of those who had served on the previous restoration committees were now themselves interred in the ground. The empty caretaker's house was symbolic of the fact that the cemetery had, indeed, no one to look after it. Only the Van Sicklen Cemetery, adjacent to the Gravesend Cemetery, was still maintained by the family, most of whom now reside outside of Gravesend.

On the basis of the words of a sign on the cemetery gate, which stated that the cemetery was under the jurisdiction of the president of the Borough of Brooklyn, I decided to begin a fourth and, hopefully, final clean-up campaign. Having helped David G. Oats for two years in projects to restore old World's Fair structures at Flushing Meadows–Corona Park in Queens, I used this experience in getting the city to undertake improvements in Gravesend.

In the course of this, I also discovered the incredible fact that this oldest of English-speaking settlements in Brooklyn, which has such an amazing panorama of history, had never had a historical society. In June 1972, therefore, I founded the Gravesend Historical Society for the purposes of preserving the unique history of the town and disseminating its history throughout the community. Local history is bread-and-butter history—the most relevant of all. Pride in the past of one's own small area increases pride in the area today. It gives residents something to be proud of and care for.

The society was established with an official seal, depicting the major elements of Gravesend's background, and a board of directors was formed, with myself as president, David Oats as vice president, Professors Arthur Konop and James Waters of the James Kelly Local Historical Studies Institute of St. Francis College and Dr. Joseph Palisi, then a history professor at St. Francis College, as historians.

The first priority and goal of the society after its official establishment was the clean-up of the cemetery. Upon investigation, it was discovered that in 1968 the cemetery was transferred from the borough president's office to the New York

City Department of Real Estate. Finding this out, the society demanded that the department clean up the grounds, restore the headstones, and maintain and keep watch over the area.

After little response from the City, in August 1972, the society held an inspection of the grounds, which was covered by the *New York Daily News*. The article revealed the deplorable state of the cemetery and in photos depicted graphically the shame of overgrown weeds and toppled tombstones. Dr. Palisi joined David Oats and me on the tour and lent his professional background as an archaeologist and historian to the effort. This opened a new phase in Dr. Palisi's career, for through his work with the Gravesend Historical Society, he was appointed the official historian of Brooklyn by Borough President Sebastian Leone in September 1973 and served that position until 1978.

The *Daily News* article of September 8, 1972, exposed the situation and brought quick response from Ira Duchan, commissioner of the Real Estate Department of the city. He stated to the *News* that the department would begin a clean-up and that "we want to do it the way the society wants it done."

With this breakthrough, slowly but surely the City began to clean out the debris. In huge piles it would be loaded into bins large enough to accept the accumulated junk of years of neglect. By October, the trees had been pruned, the weeds removed, and a number of headstones restored.

Then, a setback. Halloween, 1972, brought with it the usual pranks, but to the cemetery it brought massive vandalism. By November 1, many tombstones were overturned and broken. Dead cats, broken and mutilated dolls, and signs of burnings on tombstones suggested the work of amateur occultists. The society immediately revealed this situation to the local police and the press. An article in the *News* attributed the work to those who engage in witchcraft. This accusation was protested by Leo Martello in his book *Witchcraft: The Old Religion*. Martello attributed the accusation to prejudice and a lack of knowledge as to what present-day witches practice.

In any event, it was now evident that if the cemetery was to be preserved for all times, and not just the focal point of periodic and eventually unsuccessful clean-ups, more substantial improvements would have to be made to ensure its survival. The society requested three things from the City: 1. that special spotlights be installed to prevent future night vandalism; 2. that a caretaker once again be assigned to look after the cemetery and take care of the grounds; 3. that the Landmarks Preservation Commission officially designate the cemetery as a city landmark.

With the arrival of spring 1973, a new day came for Gravesend as residents could once again look through the newly painted fence and see the historic grounds that lay within their midst, but which many had never seen. On the first visitors day on Palm Sunday, people could once again walk through the tranquil and bucolic setting to view the markers of those who built the town. A caretaker had been assigned and made sure the grounds were well kept and manicured. At night, the frosty glow of newly installed spotlights gave a protective covering to the cemetery. The effort to restore the cemetery began the work of the new historical society and this campaign was best summed up by Louis D. Fontana in a poem called "An Obscure Labor," which he wrote after hearing of the 1972 Halloween vandalism (reprinted here with the poet's permission).

Where Gravesend Neck, McDonald meets,
An ancient village lies asleep.
Once long ago an outcast band,
Of weary trav'lers found this land,
Here far from bustling Boswijck Creek,
A simple life they sought to reap.

Lovely this long island was,
Île des Lapins, white sands and shrubs,
Salt marsh, shell snipe and flounder filled,
Secluded from high Prospect's rills.
With courage springtime soil was sown,
By summer sprang forth grain for scones,
Untrammeled here by taxes royal,
The village grew rich for its toil.

But Nieaw Amsterdam was thriving,
And Breukelen bound'ries wid'ning,
Mid wood and flat bush built to suit,
Till streets colliding choked the roots,
The village died, not much was left
Save silent tombstones to attest,
"Stalwart, we the single trace,
Beneath sleeps a forgotten race."

If some did wish to see these stones,
For sake of history, re-zoned,
They'd brave their way through thorny crowds,
Which now replace more fruitful boughs,
Or ride the "El's" great grinding hound,
That feasts on eardrums of the proud,
To reach the tablets, deftly carved,
Set well behind a huge garage.

Such obscure labor much endured,
That some memory be assured.
Then idle hands like hammers smashed,
Our precious mirrors of the past.
Be cursed forever evil pack,
That roamed at night garroting cats,
Beware! This curse be thrice on those,
Who dare despoil this just repose.

Copyright © 1973 by Louis D. Fontana.

The Gravesend Cemetery and the Van Sicklen Cemetery received landmark status on March 23, 1976. For its part, the society installed a flagpole and assisted in the restoration of many tombstones in the graveyard. At the Gravesend Cemetery ceremony, on the exact day 328 years after Governor Willem Kieft signed the charter for Gravesend, a proclamation was read by another governor, Nelson Rockefeller, who proclaimed December 19, 1973, as "Gravesend Day" in the State of New York. It was one of his last official acts as governor of New York State. As the community assembled in the auditorium, the school band and choir began to sing "the Gravesend Song," a piece written especially for the occasion to the tune of "Edelweiss."

No sooner was the new historical society instituted than new problems arose. Had the society not been formed just in the nick of time, three of the few remaining reminders of the unique history of Gravesend would have been lost forever.

DEDICATION OF THE GRAVESEND AND VAN SICKLEN CEMETERIES, 1976. From left to right, Horatio B. Suckling (from Gravesend, England), Borough President Sebastian Leone, author-historian Eric Ierardi, and Mr. Suckling's nephew participate in the unveiling.

In the summer of 1973, it became known that a private developer was about to raze the Elias Hubbard Ryder Home, located at 1926 East Twenty-Eighth Street, to construct a series of attached row homes. The home, built in 1822, was one of only three remaining structures in Gravesend from that period in history. Many local residents expressed fears that the residence would be demolished, to be replaced only by a high rise or attached structures, which have become all too typical landmarks on the urban scene.

The historical society began a campaign to save the structure from demolition. With the assistance of State Senator Donald Halperin, the society began to negotiate with Carl Mondello, the owner of the property. Mondello, it turned out, was very interested in seeing the home preserved, but had financial obligations that demanded that he sell the property. After a series of meetings with Frank Gilbert, executive director of the New York City Landmarks Preservation Commission, Mondello agreed to hold off the closing of the sale until a buyer could be found for the house, who could equal the price to be paid by the developer, or until an alternate location could be found to relocate the house.

Following the example set by the moving of the Kingsland Homestead in Flushing when it was in danger of demolition in 1968, the society, along with Gilbert, attempted to have the home moved to a site adjacent to P.S. 95 in the main "Four Square" area of the town. The board of education, which owned the site, a former "victory garden" during World War II, agreed to have the home placed on the site to be operated as a historical museum.

However, massive problems were involved in physically moving the house because of overhead telephone and electric power lines and two elevated subway lines. The crisis was averted when a private individual came forward to purchase the house for the required price. The buyer was interested in living in and preserving the Ryder Home. Additional support came when Mayor John V. Lindsay wrote to the society on July 10, 1973, saying that the Landmarks Preservation Commission had informed him "it will not be razed." The home was saved; and the Landmarks Preservation Commission designated the home a landmark on March 23, 1976.

The second crisis developed when it was discovered that the stately Parachute Jump of Coney Island was put up for bid by the City. When no one came forward to purchase it, word spread that the City would move to demolish it, or, just as bad, let it rot, unattended and open to vandals.

The society and many others, including the Coney Island Chamber of Commerce, believed that the Parachute Jump was the very symbol of Coney Island itself. The society has termed it "the Eiffel tower of Brooklyn." A thing of great beauty, it is a world-renowned landmark that represents all that Coney Island means to people across the globe. Having been a major part of the New York World's Fair of 1939–1940 before being purchased by Steeplechase Park in 1941, and being the first sight which passengers on arriving Atlantic Ocean liners see upon arrival in America (even before they see the Statue of Liberty), it is a "landmark" in the truest sense of that word. Therefore, in 1973, the society, along with the Flushing Meadows–Corona Park World's Fair Association, applied to the Landmarks Preservation Commission to designate the Parachute Jump as an official landmark, thus preserving it for future generations. Since the tower itself is in good structural condition, it was proposed by the society in its "Proposal for Gravesend's Participation in the 1976 Bicentennial of the United States Celebrations," that a beacon of welcome be installed on the top of the structure, which would no longer be operated as a "thrill ride," but would be called "Coney Island Tower." In addition, a small museum on the history of the island could be located at the base of the tower, thus preserving for the future the exciting and colorful past of this "isle by the sea." What more fitting landmark for the Bicentennial than a beacon of welcome from that first glimpse of America from the Atlantic Ocean. The Parachute Jump was designated a landmark in 1977; it was later withdrawn, and then on May 23, 1989, it was made official again.

The third Gravesend crisis occurred in 1974, when a proposal was put forward to rename Lady Moody Square, a small triangle of trees and park benches at Avenue U between Lake and Van Sicklen Streets. The family of a Stephen Turzilli, a local boy killed in Vietnam, had petitioned for the square to be renamed after the soldier. Two New York City councilmen submitted a bill in the council to effect the name change.

A storm of protest followed as the historical society objected to this desecration of Lady Moody's name. This square, adjacent to her original property, is the only official memorial to this great woman and founder of the Town of Gravesend.

The square was named in an official city council bill enacted in 1940 and signed into law by Mayor Fiorello La Guardia.

A small group of residents wished to remove the name in favor of someone else. The society said it was not against a memorial to the young man, and in fact pointed out a number of unnamed parks and playgrounds in the immediate vicinity that could bear the soldier's name. The society said it would help to see this accomplished, and also proposed placing a memorial stone or monument on Lady Moody Square in memory of local boys killed in the various wars. This was achieved many years later.

But the proponents of the name change continued their insistence that the square be renamed. The society undertook a campaign to educate the citizenry as to who Lady Moody was and her importance in Brooklyn and national history. Many groups and individuals came to support the society's fight, including the United War Veterans of King's County, the Brooklyn Historical Society, the New York City Bicentennial Corporation, the Borough Historian of Brooklyn, and the National Organization of Women.

These three crises showed the importance of having a watchdog organization over a local community interested in the preservation of the few remaining legacies of the area. Every community should have such an organization to see to it that its heritage is not destroyed by vandals from within.

The new society was also formed in time to commemorate a number of significant anniversaries. The 330th anniversary of the founding of Gravesend was marked by proclamations from Borough President Leone and Mayor Lindsay, who declared March 2, 1973, as "Gravesend Day." The mayor requested "all citizens to commemorate the 330th anniversary of Gravesend, which coincides with the 75th anniversary of Greater New York, and to bear in mind the valor of its first community." On May 7, 1974, another mayor, Abraham Beame, issued a proclamation "commemorating the 320th anniversary of the purchase of Coney Island" and declared May 7 as "Coney Island Day" in the City of New York.

Thirty years have nearly passed since the founding of the Gravesend Historical Society. The society has been successful in saving a number of historical sites and educating the general public and students through historical exhibits, audio-visual presentations, lectures, and historical publications. The battles were many and long as the society tried to save some of the remaining legacies in the community.

The Parachute Jump at Coney Island had received designation in July 1977. Shortly thereafter, the Board of Estimate, which today no longer exists, voted down the status, claiming that it would cost $1 million to restore and another $10,000 to maintain it each year. The society requested consideration and fought the City to overturn its decision. As time went on and with constant prodding, the Parachute Jump received its permanent status on May 23, 1989. A restoration program included the removal of years of rust and the painting of the jump. Electrical work included new spotlights and navigational lights atop the jump. I can still recall the hearing at the Board of Estimate, when the then park's commissioner referred to the jump as a "piece of junk." Its fate at that time seemed gloomy. Yes, well one can fight city hall after all!

Also in 1977, the society nominated the Cyclone Roller Coaster Ride to become a New York City Landmark. Among the many things stated in favor of the ride was its safety record and several historical facts. After 11 years, the City finally designated the ride a historic landmark on July 12, 1988. One year later, on May 23, 1989, Coney Island's Wonder Wheel Ferris wheel, built in 1918–1920 by the Eccentric Ferris Wheel Amusement Company, was also designated.

During the spring of 1977, the society was made aware that the Gravesend Dutch Reformed Church was about to sell its property and perhaps the church edifice demolished by its new owners. The congregation had been reduced to a point that they no longer could financially support the parish. They were about to join with another parish and cut expenses. The society was concerned with saving the building. At the time, Reverend Emanuel Greco was the pastor of the Coney Island Pentecostal Church, which was located on the southeast corner of Van Sicklen Street and Gravesend Neck Road where the Korean Christian Church is located today. Reverend Greco's congregation had grown to the point that the church no longer was able to accommodate them. He asked the society to intercede and see if the Gravesend Reformed Church would be interested in selling their property to his congregation. They were interested, and after a series of meetings, an agreement was made to sell the property. The society still desires to see this beautiful brick and terra-cotta edifice declared an official New York City Landmark.

April 1977 was a celebrated month for the Gravesend community. On April 17, the Gravesend Museum was opened at P.S. 95, the Gravesend School. The school had a spare classroom and offered it to the society as a possible site for the community museum. After much work, it was transformed into a historical museum. The opening ceremony was attended by all city officials plus community and cultural groups. The museum remained in operation for several years until an increase in enrollment warranted the return of the room for educational purposes. Many items from the historical collections of the society were placed on display in the school's auditorium, including one of the doors from Lady Moody's House, which remains on loan to the school.

During March 1979, Councillor Peter Dyke from Gravesend, England, visited its American counterpart. He had come in order to plan the forthcoming "twinning" ceremonies that were to take place between the two Gravesends. It had been decided that ceremonies would take place on both sides of the Atlantic. On June 9, 1979, a twinning ceremony took place in Gravesend, England. I represented the United States and brought with me documents from the mayor, borough president, and other local officials. An official entry was made into the Congressional Record of the United States from the 96th Congress, first session, H. Res. 294, which was entered on May 31, 1979, declaring "To designate June 9th, 1979 as 'Gravesend, Brooklyn, New York and Gravesend, England, Twin Communities' Anniversary Day.'"

THE TWINNING OF GRAVESENDS, 1979. This celebration took place at Public School 95 with an assortment of Colonial soldiers and local officials and visiting English dignitaries.

On November 30, 1979 at P.S. 95, a ceremony was held in Gravesend, Brooklyn, for the twinning of the two Gravesend communities. Many city officials were present, including former New York City mayor John V. Lindsay. His Worship, Mayor William Dyke and the Mayoress from England were present as well as former mayor Len Hardy and his wife. Horatio B. Suckling attended with some other guests from England. The delegates also visited Brooklyn's Borough Hall and Borough President Howard Golden and Manhattan's City Hall and Mayor Edward I. Koch. A sign declaring the official twinning was unveiled at the ceremony as well as a proclamation from the Lord Mayor. Men dressed as American Revolutionary soldiers saluted the dignitaries by sounding a volley of gunfire.

Gravesend received international notoriety on another occasion. It was on November 14, 1979, that one of Gravesend's own was held hostage along with 51 other United States citizens in Teheran, Iran. After 444 days of captivity, on January 20, 1981, Barry Rosen was released after an agreement between the Iranian and U.S. governments.

A ceremony was held on March 14, 1981, locally in Gravesend to honor Barry Rosen. It was my pleasure to present to him a laminated copy of the Coat of Arms of Gravesend. On this very day, all those who were present at the ceremony were reminded that Gravesend was a haven for religious freedom as well as for those who suffered some form of oppression.

During the 1980s the society continued to conduct lectures, walking tours, and historical presentations. Talks were given at the Montaulk Club, which is located in the historic Park Slope section of Brooklyn. The society continued into the 1990s to serve as a watchdog and an educational force in the community.

In October 1998, good news reached the society with the announcement of the Landmarks Preservation Commission in declaring Fire Engine Company 253 (originally Engine Company 53—later Engine Company 153) a New York City Landmark. Located on Eighty-Sixth Street and Bay Thirty-Seventh Street, it was originally built for the City of Brooklyn in 1895–1896. The two-story structure is a major work by the prominent architectural firm of Parfitt Brothers. This Bensonhurst firehouse is a rare example of the Dutch Renaissance Revival style, with similar structures built in northern Europe and the American colonies during the seventeenth century.

As Gravesend enters the twenty-first century, I am confident that the good works of the Gravesend Historical Society will continue. The society serves the community as an educational institution and as a sentinel watching and protecting its sacred treasures. Since the society's inception in 1972, many of Gravesend's citizens have become mindful of the community's history. More and more people have become more respectful of Gravesend's past and have taken a greater pride in the neighborhood.

The educational plan set by the historical society has worked. The new Asian and Russian immigrants will, as they assimilate, learn to respect and understand the history of their new community, just as the previous Italian and Jewish immigrants did. In the future, Gravesend will continue to be a safe and enjoyable community. It will continue to be a haven for immigrants and will continue to serve as a retreat for those that enjoy freedom of religion and the freedom to live in peace.

ROSEN CELEBRATION, 1981. Eric Ierardi (left) presents former Iran hostage Barry Rosen (right) with a Gravesend's Coat of Arms upon his return to Gravesend.

155

BIBLIOGRAPHY

BOOKS

Armburster, Eugene L. *Coney Island*.

Bergen, Teunis. *The Early Settlers of Kings County*. Long Island, NY: reprinted, Cottonport, LA: Polyonthos, 1973.

Bliven, Bruce, and Naomi Bliven. *New York, The Story of the World's Most Exciting City*. New York: Random House, 1969.

Bonner, William T. *New York World's Metropolis*. New York: New York City Directory, R.L. Polk & Co., 1924.

Botkin, B.A. *New York City Folklore*. New York: Random House, 1956.

Broadhead, John. *Documents Relative to the Colonial History of the State of New York*.

Colonial History, *Declarations Concerning Depredations on Long Island*. Vol. 14.

Condon, Thomas J. *New York Beginnings: The Commercial Origins of New Netherland*. New York: New York U.P., 1968.

Ditmas, Charles A. *Historic Homesteads of Kings County*. Brooklyn: the Compiler, 1909.

Dowd, Willis Bruce. *The Measures of Meal*. Boston: Riverdale Press, 1910.

Eberlein, Harold Donaldson. *Manor Houses and Historic Homes of Long Island and Staten Island*. Philadelphia: J.P. Lippincott.

Emerson, Caroline D. *New York City—Old and New*. New York: Dutton & Co., 1953.

Fernow, Berthold. *New York in the Revolution*. New York: Board of Regents, NY State Archives, 1887.

Field, Thomas W. *The Battle of Long Island*. Brooklyn: L.I. Historical Society, 1869.

Flint, M.B. *Early Long Island*.

Franklin, Joe. *Classics of the Silent Screen*. New York: Citadel.

Furman, Gabriel. *Antiques of Long Island*.

Gabriel, R.H. *The Evolution of Long Island*. 1960.

Goodwin, Maud W. *Historic New York*. Vol. 2. New York: Privately Printed, 1899.

Handlin, Oscar. *The Newcomers*. Cambridge: Harvard U.P., 1959.

Hervey, John. *Racing and Breeding in America and the Colonies*. London: London Press, 1931.

History of Coney Island. New York: Burroughs & Co., 1904.

Huntington, Edna. *Historical Markers and Monuments in Brooklyn*. Brooklyn: L.I. Historical Society, 1952.

Jacobs, Lewis. *The Rise of the American Film*. New York: Teachers College Press, Columbia University, 1968.

Johnston, Henry P. *The Campaign of 1776 around New York and Brooklyn*. Brooklyn: L.I. Historical Society, 1878.

Jones, Rufus. *The Quakers in the American Colonies*. New York: Norton, 1966.

Kelley, Frank Bergen. *Historical Guide to the City of New York*. New York: Frederick A. Stokes Co., 1913.

Kessler, Henry H. and Eugene Rachles. *Peter Stuyvesant and His New York*. New York: Random House, 1959.

Knickerbocker, Diedrick. *A History of New York from the Beginning of the World to the End of the Dutch Dynasty*.

Lamarque, Abril, and John Richmond. *Brooklyn U.S.A.* New York: Creative Press, 1946.

Lauber, Gilber, and Samuel Kaplan. *The New York City Handbook*. New York: Doubleday, 1966.

Leopold, Carl. *Baurmerster's Journal*. Translated and annotated by Bernhard A. Uhlendorf. Rutgers U.P., 1957.

Longrigg, Roger. *The History of Horse Racing*. New York: Stein and Day, 1972.

Lossing, Benson J. *Field Book of the American Revolution*. New York: Harper and Brothers, 1850–52.

Mangels, William F. *The Outdoor Amusement Industry*. New York: Vantage Press, 1952.

McCollough, Edo. *Good Old Coney Island*. New York: Charles Scribner's Sons, 1957.

Morell, Parker. *Diamond Jim*. New York: Simon and Schuster, 1934.

Morison, Samuel Eliot. *The European Discovery of America, The Northern Voyages*. New York: Oxford U.P., 1971.

Moses, Robert. *Public Works: A Dangerous Trade*. New York: McGraw-Hill, 1969.

Murphy, Mark, and F. Weld. *Treasury of Brooklyn*. New York: William Sloane Publishers, 1945.

Nevins, Allan, and John A. Krout. *The Greater City: New York 1898–1948*. New York: Columbia U.P., 1948.

New York City Guide. New York: Federal Writers Project, Random House, 1939.

O'Callaghan, E.B. *The Documentary History of the State of New York*. Albany: Weed, Parsons, 1849.

Onderdonk, Henry. *Revolutionary Incidents of Suffolk and Kings Counties*.

Ostrander, Stephen M. *A History of the City of Brooklyn and Kings County*. Brooklyn: 1894.

Overton, Jacqueline. *Long Island's Story*. New York: Doubleday Doran, 1932.

Pennypacker, Morton. *General Washington's Spies on Long Island and in New York*. Brooklyn: L.I. Island Historical Society, 1939.

Pilat, Oliver, and Jo Ranson. *Sodom By the Sea*. New York: Garden City Publishing, 1943.

Prime, N.S. *A History of Long Island*. New York and Chicago: Lewis Publishing, 1905.

Raesly, Ellis L. *Portrait of New Netherland*. 1945.

Rambles about Historic Brooklyn. Brooklyn: the Brooklyn Trust, 1916.

Rosenwaike, Ira. *Population History of New York City*. New York: Syracuse U.P., 1972.

Ross, Peter. *A History of Long Island*. New York: Lewis Publishing, 1902.

Seymann, Jerrold. *Colonial Charters, Patents and Grants to the Communities Comprising the City of New York*. New York: the Board of Statutory Consolidation of New York, 1939.

Short History of New York State. New York: Cornell U.P., 1957.

Smith, Albert E. *Two Reels and a Crank*. New York: Doubleday, 1952.

Smith, Thomas E.V. *The City of New York*. Riverside, CT: Chatham Press, 1972.

Stiles, Henry R. *A History of Kings County*. New York: W.W. Munsell & Co., 1884.

Szasz, Suzanne, and Susan E. Lyman. *Young Folk's New York*. New York: Crown, 1960.

Thompson, B.F. *History of Long Island*.

Thompson, John H. *Geography of New York State*. New York: Syracuse U.P., 1966.

Van Der Donck, Adraen. *A Description of the New Netherlands*. New York: Syracuse U.P., 1968.

Van Voorhees, Elias W. *A Geology of the Van Voorhees Family in America*.

Van Wyck, Frederick. *Keskachauge or the First White Settlement on Long Island*. New York: G.S. Putnam & Sons, 1924.

Vosburg, William S. *Racing in America 1866–1921*.

Weld, Ralph F. *Brooklyn is America*. New York: Columbia U.P., 1950.

Wheeler, Richard. *Voices of 1776*. New York: Thomas Y. Crowell Co., 1972.

Williamson, W.M. *Adrian Block, Navigator, Fur Trader, Explorer—New York's First Shipbuilder*. New York: Marine Museum of the City of New York, 1959.

Wilson, James Grant. *The Memorial History of the City of New York*. New York: New York History Co., 1892.

Wilson, R.R. *New York Old and New, Its Story, Streets, and Landmarks*. New York: Privately Printed, 1909.

Wood, Silas. *A Sketch of the First Settlement of the Several Towns on Long Island with their Political Condition to the End of the Revolution*. Brooklyn: Alden Spooner, 1828.

ARTICLES

Adams, C.F. "The Battle of Long Island." *American Historical Review*. 1896.

Flick, Alexander C. "Lady Deborah Moody, Grand Dame of Gravesend." *The L.I. Historical Quarterly*, I (No. 3), July 1939.

Hasler, P.W. "The History of Parliment: The House of Commons: 1558–1603." *The Genealogist*. (No. 29).

Platt, Isabelle. "An Old Colonial Homestead Born Again." *Country Life in America*. XVI (No. 2), June 1909.

Wiltshire Archeological and Natural History Magazine. (No. 60), December 1913.

Wiltshire Notes and Queries. (No. 7), March 1915.

NEWSPAPERS

The *Brooklyn Eagle*

The *New York Herald Tribune*

The *New York Journal-American*

The *New York Mirror*

The *New York News*

The *New York Recorder*

The *New York Times*

The *New York Tribune*

The *World*

PRIMARY SOURCE MATERIALS

The Gravesend Town Records
Indian Deeds of Gravesend
Purchase of Coney Island Document
Town Charters of Gravesend
Town Plan of Gravesend
William Dunch's Will (Shire Hall, County Registry Office, Reading, Berkshire)

The above material (except for William Dunch's will) is housed at the James A. Kelly Local Historical Studies Institute of Saint Francis College in Brooklyn. The material is on permanent loan from the County Clerk's Office of Kings County.

MISCELLANEOUS

Borough of Brooklyn's Annual Reports
Department of Parks Annual Reports
"Gravesend," published by the *Brooklyn Eagle*.
Gravesend Historical Notes. The James A Kelly Local Historical Studies Institute and County Clerk's Office.
Kerr, Reverend Kenneth Howard. "The 300th Anniversary of the Gravesend Reformed Church." 1955.
New York City Plan and Survey Committee Finances and Financial Administration of New York City, 1928.
New York City Department of Health Annual Reports of the Board of Health.
New York City Planning Commission. "The Plan for New York City," Section 3, Brooklyn. 1969.
New York Secretary of State Census of the State of New York for 1855.
United States Department of Commerce Census Reports.
Van Voorhees, Dr. Oscar. "Historical Handbook of the Van Voorhees Family in the Netherlands and America." 1935.

INDEX